Here is your Breakthrough Language Learning CD.

Use it in conjunction with this book.

The CD is packed with invaluable exercises, tips and memory tricks to help you learn your new language in record time.

We don't recommend you play it while driving because it's interspersed with exercises that would take your attention off the road.

Better to play it somewhere you can sit down and concentrate. There will also be some points where you may want to pause your CD to give you time to think or to make notes on what we are telling you.

The CD has **four** main sections, each split into a number of steps and containing **20 steps** in total.

The **first section** helps you understand yourself and how you learn best.

The **second section** gives you some useful study skills.

The **third section** gives you some specific communication skills.

The **fourth section** contains a visualisation exercise, designed to help you activate your mind more effectively.

We hope you enjoy what you hear.

Published in UK in 2007 by
Rockwell House Ltd
www.rockwellhouse.co.uk

Every effort has been made to obtain the necessary permissions with reference to copyright material, both illustrative and quoted; should there be any omissions in this respect we apologise and shall be pleased to make the appropriate acknowledgements in any future edition.

ISBN 978-1-906060-00-8

Printed and bound in Great Britain by Biddles Ltd, King's Lynn, Norfolk

Breakthrough Language **Learning**

A step-by-step guide to help you master
any new language quickly and easily!

Carol Harris • Katrina Patterson • Penny Vingoe

ROCKWELLHOUSE

Contents

Introduction
Transform your language learning ability

How this book will help you learn the language of your choice, even if you've tried before and not succeeded - the twenty-step plan for success.

What's in it for you?

This book will give you techniques to transform your learning skills quickly and enjoyably. When you follow the programme contained in the book you will:

- Find out how people learn new things.
- Understand your own best ways of learning.
- Set your own goals for language learning.
- Learn how to choose the best times of day to study.
- Be able to learn at your own pace and when it's best for you.
- Improve your speaking and communication skills (useful in your own native language too).
- Improve your memory skills.
- Understand how technology can help you learn.
- Be able to apply your new knowledge to learning the language of your choice.
- Also be able to communicate better in your own language.

Some of the specific things you will be able to do with the help of this book are:

- Learn about another culture.
- Improve your job prospects.
- Enjoy holidays more than superficially.
- Be seen as an achiever.
- Expand the number of people you can communicate with.
- Help someone else.
- Be more effective as part of a multi-lingual project.

- Grow and develop.
- Enjoy life more.
- Be able to communicate with a special friend.
- Make a difference.

If even one of these means something to you, then this book is for you. What if you have tried learning before but not been successful? You may have tried learning a language before, but not succeeded and now you have the opportunity to learn tried and tested ways of ensuring success.

There are lots of reasons why people don't find it easy to learn; for example:

- They may have had bad memories of a school experience of learning languages.
- They may have expected too much from themselves too early on.
- They may have selected a learning process that isn't right for them (for example going to evening classes when they are too tired to concentrate).
- They may have chosen a time when they had too much else to do and couldn't make the progress they wanted.
- They may have believed that a learning difference (such as dyslexia) prevented them from learning.

This book will show you the best way for you to learn and give you ideas and techniques to speed up your progress. The book is split into sections that take you through a simple system for learning - you may want to pick and choose from them but, for most people, it will work best when you follow the steps as they are presented in the book.

Part One helps you identify your own motivation and learning styles.

Part Two takes you through the stages you need to follow in order to learn a new language easily and enjoyably.

Part Three gives you specific skills for learning to communicate effectively with native speakers of the language you have chosen.

Throughout the book you will find activities and exercises that back up the instructional points. There is also an accompanying CD that covers the key activities in the book, adds some new activities and gives you a visualisation exercise designed to help you relax and imagine yourself learning quickly and well. It's up to you how you use the book and CD.

We recommend you work through it in the order it is presented but, if you wish, you can skip sections, move ahead to the communications section, go back over earlier sections again and so forth. Do whatever works best for you.

And if you have a disability, you can still learn a language, even if you are dyslexic, hard of hearing or have poor vision. Everyone can learn - the only question is: "Which approach is right for you?"

Here's an example of how someone learned quickly:

Jane was notoriously bad at languages at school - at the bottom of her class. Her worst subject was German. She simply believed that she was not good at learning languages. In her mid-20s, she made friends with, and grew close to, a Greek. Her Greek friend spoke no English, but did speak German. In order to communicate with him, she became really interested in learning the words she needed to communicate sufficiently. Her German speaking ability increased beyond recognition in a matter of weeks and one reason for this is probably that when our emotions are involved, we learn faster.

So let's make a start and help you learn quickly and easily too.

A Chinese pictogram for learning
(2 concepts - studying and practising constantly)

Section One
Understanding your motivation and learning styles

Step One
Knowing your purpose

One of the most important things about language learning is to decide from the very start why you want to learn the language you select.

It may sound obvious, but imagine you want to go on a train journey and you get to the station to buy your ticket and, when the ticket clerk asks you where you want to go, you just say: "I'd like a nice day out". It would be hard for the person to sell you a ticket as you hadn't been specific about what you wanted. To reach a new place, you need to have your destination in mind.

The same is true with language learning. People can have very different reasons for wanting to learn languages and, once you know your purpose, it is so much easier to achieve the result you want.

Here are some reasons for learning; which of them apply to you? Take a few minutes to read the list and then choose those reasons that are right for you. If your own particular reason isn't on this list, just add it - the important thing is that you identify why you personally want to learn. So here goes…

I want to learn a new language

- So that I can go on holiday and be able to use some common phrases when I want to talk to people - I just want to learn the basics.
- Because I am going to live abroad and I need to be able to communicate with people there - I want a working knowledge so I can get on with day-to-day communications.
- Because I need a second language in my new job and I have to be fluent in it fairly rapidly.
- Because I need specific understanding of business or technical terminology.

- Because I have a new partner from another country and I want to be able to speak his/her language.
- Because I want to be able to help my children with their language homework - I just need to know enough to keep up with what they are being taught at school.
- I have friends or relatives overseas and want to be able to read and understand the letters or emails they send me - I don't need speaking skills but do want to read well in the language I choose.
- I want to be able to add some items in different languages to my email newsletters.
- For another reason of my own.

So you can see that reasons for learning can vary considerably, and so can the level of fluency that people need.

Some want just the basics, while others need much more depth of learning. Some need general language skills, while others need very specific ones, such as technical terminology. Some need conversational skills while others need business ones. And some people want to learn one language while others may need to learn several.

Whatever your reason, this book will help you achieve your objectives so you can speak the language you choose easily and fluently.

And, once you have your overall purpose for learning a language, you will need some additional goals - we cover this in step six.

EXERCISE
Creating a storyboard

Take a large sheet of paper and, on it, write down your overall goal for learning the language, the time-scale you believe is appropriate and the level of results you would like.

You can either write this as a list or in diagrammatic form - for example little bubbles each containing one of the goals.

Then add pictures to your sheet of paper. Pick anything that you think relates to your goals - for example a picture of someone wearing clothes of the culture you are studying, or food from the country where the language is spoken, or a picture of an aeroplane that will take you there, or a picture of a poster advertising a film in that language.

Keep your sheet of paper somewhere you will be able to see it each day - this will help keep you on track and remind you of your goals - and the pictures will help your mind remember to keep you motivated and on track.

EXERCISE
Imagining your results

Create a really clear, imaginary, picture in your mind, now. (If you think you have problems in making images, just describe your front door out loud. As you do so, you can become aware that, in some way, you do have a mental representation of the front door. It may not be very clear, but you are aware of it. Just use the same process to create the imaginary picture we are about to describe to you.)

Imagine you are engaging in a conversation with a native speaker. You are confident, you are finding the words you want to find, and you are being understood. You are enjoying understanding what is being said too - through vocabulary and through watching the body language of the speaker.

Make this image clear in your mind, make it colourful, and then be aware of being fully involved in the picture (as you experience that picture, notice that if you look down in your mental picture, you can see your shoes)!

'Tweak' the picture - make it really what you want it to be. Notice how you are speaking easily and fluently. Feel the sense of achievement, and notice how good it feels. Dwell on that feeling!

When you have done this effectively, seeing the pictures and feeling the feelings - and hearing the words you are using, then your mind will think you have done it already! And, as you know, if you have done something really well once, it is so simple to do it really well next time!

Key learning points from step one

- Have an overall purpose for your learning
- Have a time-scale for achievement
- Have a standard to work towards
- Create a 'storyboard' to remind you of where you want to be
- Visualise your goals in your mind

Step Two
Knowing your own beliefs
Finding out which beliefs can hold you back and which ones can lead you forward

Many people would be brilliant learners if only they didn't believe they couldn't do it!

Some of the things that hold people back are:
- Believing that learning is hard.
- Believing that learning is dull.
- Believing that they are poor learners.
- Believing that their memory is not good.
- Believing that it is embarrassing to practise speaking in another language.

This part of the book will tackle such beliefs and show you that learning can be fun, fast and easy.

Let's take your beliefs about learning first. Compare the methods you may have tried with the new methods we are about to introduce to you.

1) Language learning methods you may have tried and some negative outcomes you may have experienced with them
(all these learning methods may, of course, also have positive benefits)

Went to formal classes	*Drilling/learning grammar by rote (Je suis, Tu es, Il/elle est, etc). Not interesting.*
Teacher put words on a board	*You copied the words. No Discussion, no learning.*
Told to read out phrases in front of other students	*Got it wrong, others sniggered. Too embarrassed to continue.*
Read phrase books	*'How much is that hat?' (boring).*

Read new words and attempted to memorise them	*No structure. Hard work.*
Listened to tapes	*Easier, but no context. Topics not interesting.*
Weekend immersion course	*Had no idea at all what anything that was being said was about. Gave up.*

2) Language learning methods you are about to experience

Which appeals to you more - your 'old' methods or the ones we have shown you here. Which do you think we are going to present to you in this book? We believe the learning methods you are about to experience will work best for you…..

Now let's explain a bit more about beliefs.

Henry Ford has been quoted so often as saying 'If you believe you can, and you believe you can't, you are right'.

How can that be? Because we create our own beliefs. Let's explain.

Every experience we have is registered through our senses - the main five being seeing, hearing, feeling, tasting and smelling. Although our brains apparently register everything we experience, in practice, we process our experiences in various ways in order to make sense of our world.

First, we **delete** some of the information we receive from our experience - or in other words leave some of it out. This is because we can only take in so much at any one time. Just imagine consciously registering everything around you at this moment (all the details of the place you are in, all the sounds around you, the temperature of the air, the clothes you are wearing and so on. You couldn't take it all in, so you focus on some elements while ignoring others).

Then we **'filter'** some of that information - filtering being the term used for considering information according to our place of origin, our previous experience, our sensory preferences, our desires and so forth.

For instance someone born in Africa will have different filters from someone born in Britain (we don't look out for snakes in the grass beneath our feet in the same way that some of our African friends do); someone who is male will have different filters from someone who is female; someone who has been exposed to lots of languages from birth will have a different response to languages from someone who hasn't; and someone looking to buy a particular make of car will suddenly notice a remarkably large number of them on the roads.

And then we **generalise** that information - we take one experience and generalise it out to another. For example: "I had difficulty understanding what that Italian person said so I must be no good at languages....".

The following diagram illustrates these three ways of processing information: deleting, filtering and generalising.

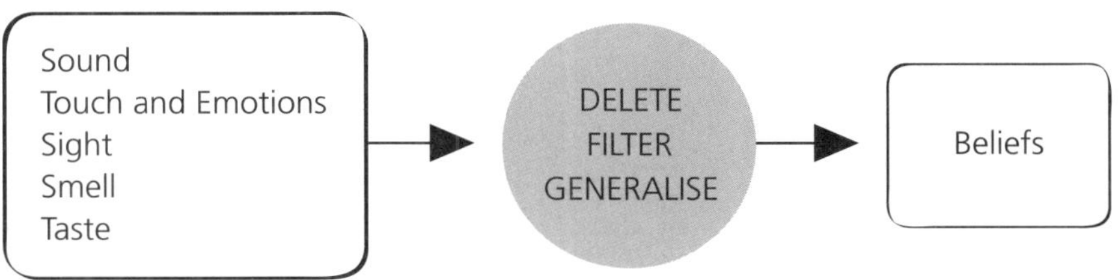

Each one of these three information processing methods results in us developing responses to circumstances including, in particular, our beliefs.

Now think it through. You have come up with your own deletions, filters and generalisations and, because you have produced them in your own head, it follows that you can also change them. So, before you start to learn a new language, it's useful to examine your beliefs about this activity.

EXERCISE

Checking the source of your beliefs about language learning and starting to change those beliefs

Take a piece of paper and jot down all the beliefs you have had about learning languages - good and bad. Maybe something like:

- I have had the belief that I simply can't learn languages.
- I have had the belief that my memory isn't as good as it used to be...
- I have had the belief that it's too big a task to learn another language.
- I have had the belief that having dyslexia makes me unable to learn well. *(By the way, if you have dyslexia in English it may not show up in another language!)*

Having created that list, ask yourself (and be honest).

- "What is the origin of this belief?" (Your answer may be, for example, that you were bottom of your class in languages at school).
- "What is the reason I still have this belief?" (Here, for example, you might say that you have never managed to learn a language to your satisfaction so far.)
- "If this belief is not useful, am I prepared to change this belief?" (The 'correct' answer to this question should be 'Yes'.)
- "What would be a more useful belief to have?"(Your answer might be that you have, in the past, been able to hold an intelligent conversation in French with a visitor to this country and that you obviously can learn a different language.)

Now you may begin to consider your beliefs about making mistakes: So do you have any of these beliefs about making mistakes?

- They are embarrassing.
- They make you look a fool.
- They show that you are not intelligent.
- They make people laugh at you.

Instead of these beliefs, what would it be like if you held the belief that if a learner can't make a mistake s/he can't make anything.

As if you were putting on a new hat, try this belief on for size. What does it feel like? Is it a belief you can accept?

Add to that belief the belief that to make mistakes is the quickest way to learn. Learning how to juggle three balls is an excellent example of learning how we have to make mistakes in order to learn. You need to drop the balls occasionally as part of the process of learning.

By experiencing mistakes, your unconscious mind registers all the ways 'not' to do things and adds them to its armoury of 'learned connections'. To understand learned connections, we need to explore a little bit about how your brain learns.

This is a diagram of one of the billions of brain cells (neurons) you have in your head.

The Axon of any one brain cell will reach out and the synaptic knob (on the end of the Axon) will connect with one of the many dendrites of another brain cell in order to create a connection.

Our brain cells actively search out other brain cells to connect with. And the number of brain cells we have is irrelevant - we have more than enough.

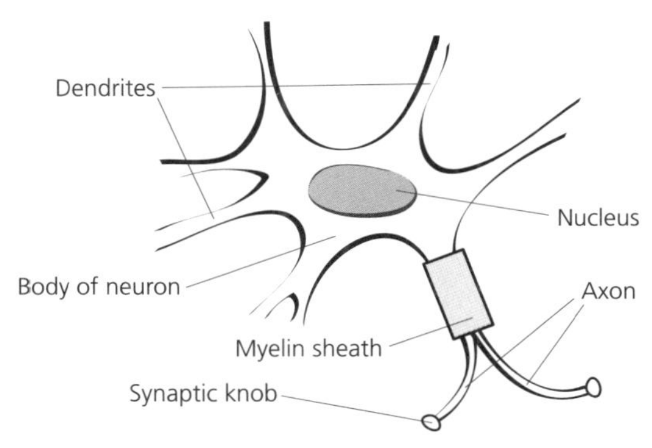

Every new experience of language, or thought about language, will create yet another connection and enhance our ability to learn. The brain physically increases in size, and increases its learning power, the more we use it and this continues until we die.

So - the more you learn, the easier it is to learn.

EXERCISE

Assessing and changing your beliefs about learning your chosen language

The interesting thing about human beings is that we can change our beliefs more easily than we think we can, and we do develop new beliefs over time - just think back to early memories - for example, Father Christmas, the tooth fairy, Elijah visiting or any other one you can think of.

Here's a list of statements that may be useful to you. Take each one and give it a number from 1 to 10 where:

10 = I absolutely believe this.

1 = I find this extremely difficult to believe.

If you think you can, you can

This is an old saying (Henry Ford again!), but very true. Focus on the positive. Self-belief is the start. If however, you think you can't, you may need some additional help.

If what you are doing doesn't work, do something different

Flexibility is the key to effectiveness; if you vary your learning methods until you get the result you want, you are more likely to be effective than if you continue trying to learn in the same way that isn't getting you results.

Patterns

There are patterns to our native language (grammar, sounds and rhythms) that organise our experience and if we change the language we speak we change these patterns - and our experience changes with them. This also means that we can have a different identity in our new language.

Learning a new language is good for your health

Your mental attitude affects your body, your health and learning and, in turn, how you behave can change your thinking. So whatever you do contributes to your overall well-being and learning a language can expand both your mental and physical horizons.

If something is possible for one person, it is possible for anybody

We have all learnt our native language naturally; mostly without learning grammar and without doing lots of homework. Throughout this book you will find case histories of people who have surprised themselves with their language learning ability and it is possible for you too.

Everyone has all the resources they need to learn another language

People have within themselves a vast reservoir of abilities and attributes; achievement is generally more about what you bring to a situation than about external elements. We have all learnt our mother tongue because our brains have the understanding of basic grammar, so we can apply this to learning a new language.

There is no failure, only feedback

If you don't achieve what you set out to do, this can provide useful information to help in your future endeavours, rather than as evidence that you are incapable of learning a second language. So notice which learning techniques do or don't work for you and adjust them accordingly.

Now, in order to make a change, discover what happens to your language learning - and your life - if you simply 'act as if' the statements above were true.

Have a go - try adopting these beliefs today! You may stretch yourself to achieve more than you ever thought possible.

Revisit this list again after you've been learning your chosen language for a couple of months and notice whether your beliefs about your own ability to learn languages has changed.

Key learning points from step two
- We all have positive and negative beliefs
- Our beliefs are created by the ways in which we perceive the world
- We can change our beliefs
- Making mistakes can help us to learn
- Our brain gives us the 'technology' for making changes to our beliefs

Step Three
Getting into a good state for learning

It's important to be in a positive state before you start to learn

An expert with the wonderful name of Mihaly Csikszentmihalyi observed that we learn much better if we are in a 'flow' state - that is when we are not bored by what we are learning, but neither are we so confused that we are put off: when we have sufficient challenge to energise us, but not so much as to overwhelm us, and when we are rested rather than stressed.

Csikszentmihalyi was reiterating what so many learning experts have discovered; that if we are in the right 'state' our learning will be much enhanced.

It is important to be in the 'right' state in order to learn and, in fact, you can choose to change the state you are in, which we will come to in the rest of this chapter.

So, what is 'a state' and what is the 'right' state for you? A 'state' is said to be make up of what you think, feel in your body and do with your body, but it's simpler to just think of it as the way you feel. For example, do you need to be interested - or fascinated? Do you need to be confident - or blasé? Do you need to be curious - or observant? Whatever works for you is the state it would be useful to choose.

ACTIVITY

- Choose an appropriate state that you want to be in every time you start doing your language learning - for this example we will use 'Confidence'.
- Think back to a time when you felt confident - and it doesn't have to have anything to do with language learning.
- Create a picture in your mind of that time when you were feeling confident. As you see the picture, notice how good it felt and even feel the feelings that you felt at that time. (See if you can notice where those feelings are in your body.)
- In your mind, listen to what people around you were saying - and indeed what you were saying to yourself.
- Make your mental picture clear, focussed and colourful; listen to the sounds and, in particular, feel those feelings.
- Come back now to the page of the book you were reading and let the mind pictures disappear.
- Now, just to test, go back to that incident in your mind and re-live it yet again - notice how good it makes you feel.
- Come back, again, to this page of the book.

The purpose of this activity is to illustrate that you can choose to re-live any feelings you have experienced in your life and you will already have experienced most of the positive feelings that we have talked about. If for any reason you can't think of a positive feeling at the moment, then just imagine what one would feel like. You might even think of someone who seems always to be that way - imagine a friend (or someone on the TV) who is always confident (or whichever other state you want to create) and pretend you are that person - imagining what s/he feels like.

Every time you start one of your learning sessions, ensure that you have chosen one of the positive states and re-visited it, so that you are once again in that state and therefore much more able to learn effectively.

Be aware of your body

Being aware of your body is an important aid to learning. Here are some aspects of body awareness and development that you might like to work on:

> ### EXERCISE
>
> Researchers tell us that exercise encourages our brains to work at optimum capacity. They tell us that it helps our nerve cells to multiply, strengthening their interconnections and protecting them from damage. Certainly it causes our hearts to work harder, thus pushing oxygen around the body - and that makes us more alert. If you have space, a baby trampoline is helpful; any time you feel 'stuck', bounce for five minutes and you should be in a much better state to continue. You can also do some 'brain gym' - see Appendix.
>
> ### Breathing
>
> Slow, deep, abdominal breathing aids learning and quietens the mind. Deep breathing enables you to get vital oxygen around your body, so remember to breathe! Because people who visualise a lot tend to breathe more shallowly, if this applies to you, you will need to pay particular attention to deepening your breathing. If you spend long hours at the computer you'll notice that your breathing gets shallow as you tend to forget to breathe well.

When you are fully absorbed in something with a sense of flow (see earlier in this section), your breathing automatically deepens, but you tend not to notice this happening.

Food and water

Your brain needs nutrients, as does your body, so you should eat a balanced diet, including protein, complex carbohydrates and fats, making sure you have plenty of vegetables (especially bright or dark coloured ones) and fruit. And you should also make sure you drink plenty of water.

Although people differ in their views on the usefulness of food supplements, some that are often recommended to help brain function are Ginko Biloba for memory and fish/plant oils containing Omega 3 fatty acids for concentration.

Relaxation

When you are undertaking a study session at home, learning new words, or assimilating what you have learned so far, periods of relaxation will give your mind some vital 'down-time' (although during that time your mind is still processing).

So take a break of 20 minutes every hour and a half and also use your judgment to take additional five-minute breaks whenever necessary.

In 1953, researchers Aserinksy and Kleitman (USA) discovered that the body's Basic Rest and Activity Cycle (BRAC) that runs throughout our 24-hour cycle is 90 to 120 minutes of activity followed by 20 minutes of rest. Rapid Eye Movement (REM) takes place during the rest periods, both during the day and night, and seems to be important for long term memory and learning at a cellular level. (See The 20-Minute Break - Appendix).

I'm just taking some 'down time'

Sleep

Learn how much sleep you need in order to operate at your best and make sure you take it. At night, your nervous system is working on what has been going on in your head during the day - keeping some and dumping what is no longer required and you may find that, by the morning, you have solutions to problems you have had, or have absorbed pieces of learning you undertook the day before.

Posture

Faulty perception often leads us to think that we are comfortable when we are slumped or scrunched into an unusual position. The spine is like a super-highway allowing information to move quickly around the body and when you slump the energy supply to various parts is blocked and learning suffers. Be aware of your posture. There are several techniques for improving body posture and usage, for example Alexander Technique, Feldenkrais and Pilates and you may want to explore some of these.

'Self talk'

What you say to yourself inside your head reflects your beliefs and changes your state. We speak out loud at about 125 words per minute and we can think to ourselves at about 500 words per minute - so fast we are hardly aware of how we can undermine ourselves.

EXERCISE

Take five minutes to write down everything you are saying to yourself in relation to your language learning. Is what you have written true and valid? Experiment with the tone of voice that you use to talk to yourself - loud and encouraging is good - and add some stirring music. If you have something negative to say to yourself, use a fast cartoon voice, or make the voice ridiculously slow.

INTERESTING FACT

Peptides (amino-acids) are one form of neuro-transmitters. They move around our body, brain and nervous system. Peptides modulate emotions and carry information - transmitting memories of learned experiences around the body. Also, when the brain makes new connections, your body stores this information. This helps explain a little of what happens when you learn a new language.

CASE HISTORY

Helen (28) left school with few qualifications and found herself a job grooming horses. Her love of horses took her to work in a stables in Germany.

While working in a bar to make extra money she surprised herself with how much of the language she had picked up through total immersion. One day, when looking out of a train window at a long station name, she realised that she could picture the whole word easily. She seemed to be able to spell in German but not in English.

As a result of her school experience her self-confidence was low, but she took herself off to a German evening class and was soon speaking German with ease and passing exams. This made her think: "If I can do this now, what else can I do?". Back in the UK and curious, Helen took a test and found that she did indeed have dyslexia, which had caused her to struggle at school. With her confidence boosted and the German language qualification as a passport, she trained as an air hostess - a dream come true.

Key learning points from step three

- Develop some good learning states
- You have access to an incredible variety of states
- What you think, feel and do has a huge effect on how you learn - keep it positive
- Your habitual ways of thinking and making decisions affect: a) the way you prefer to learn a new language and b) how you relate to others in both your own and your chosen language
- Your body needs exercise, food, water and relaxation

Step Four
Understanding your own motivation

We are all different - and we will be expanding on this in the next couple of sections! As we have already mentioned, one of the reasons we are different is that we 'filter' the experiences we have.

The filters we use are numerous, for example one person may look for detail when seeing a room for the first time, while another may take in the whole ambience.

We all have our own personal preferences too - for example some people prefer 'hotter' food than others - and these responses are also each on a continuum so that, for example, a plate of curry might be very spicy to one person, a little spicy to another, fairly mild to another and very mild to another; it isn't a question of just 'either/or'.

These differences are relevant to people types as well. Our preferences and motivations make us differ from each other and, if we are able to recognise different 'people types', we can better understand ourselves. This, in turn, helps us use the knowledge about ourselves as individuals to make learning another language easier.

Here are some useful examples of differences between people. In the examples, we do show extremes but remember that each example is actually on a continuum - or 'sliding scale' - and that you could easily have a bit of both ends of the spectrum built into your personality.

And, we are - for the sake of simplicity - referring to people as if they always demonstrated one or other of the preferences, but in fact they can vary over time and from one situation to another. So here are the examples:

Proactive or reactive

A proactive person will go in and 'make it happen' - often with little thought for the consequences. If you are learning a language this is very useful because you will simply go and talk - and practise - and may well benefit from the experience.

A reactive person is more likely to wait until the situation is 'right' - you may feel the need to learn some vocabulary before daring to go and communicate with native speakers. While this sort of person may not gain the benefits of 'just doing', if it makes you more comfortable then it is the style to adopt.

Toward or away from

A 'toward' person is much more likely to benefit from setting goals because their focus is about achieving specific things. If you are this sort of person, aim to talk to a certain number of native speakers by Friday, or learn 50 words in the next two weeks. A 'toward' person really gets motivated by having something to achieve by a certain time.

If you are an 'away from' person you are more likely to notice what it would be better not to do. You notice the problems and your focus is on solving those problems. So, for the language learner, you may recognise that you can't go and talk to someone unless you have some key words, so you will be motivated to learn basic vocabulary before going out to talk to native speakers. The 'away from' trait is useful because it makes you more likely to be a perfectionist when learning new words - and to recognise when words are spoken or spelled incorrectly.

Internal or external

If you have internal referencing, you are more inclined to decide for yourself what you need to do, or not do. You will collect information from a book like this, but you will decide for yourself whether what we say is useful - or not - and will act accordingly. It will not worry you if you make errors when talking to native speakers - although you will notice and choose to change - or not!

If you are externally referenced you like feedback. Other people's opinions matter to you and can help you, so when learning a language it is good for you to have someone with you who will comment on how you are doing. You need to have someone else help you to set goals and timetables and maybe even to be there to give you 'reminders' by asking how you are doing. With encouragement you will thrive!

Options and procedures

If you are an 'options' person you will always be looking for ways in which you can do things differently. You will look for, and find, ways in which you can get to talk to native speakers - that there aren't any around won't bother you - you will find native speakers on the computer or find someone who knows someone who knows someone... You are excited by the prospect of finding a 'different' way to do things.

If you are a 'procedures' person you are more inclined to learn through having set rules to follow. You will find learning grammar easy. It is directive and specific and something you can 'hold on to'; you will know you are doing it 'right'. You will probably also like working through a textbook consistently. However, procedures usually start somewhere and end somewhere else. Learning a language does not have an 'end', for you can continue to learn for the rest of your life. You need therefore to set yourself specific grammar, vocabulary, or other tasks that you can follow through and get satisfaction through completing.

General or specific

If you have a 'general' pattern, you like an overview of a subject, but may not be so good at getting into the detail of it. You are likely to understand concepts easily and to be able to put a language into its cultural framework quite easily. The 'immersion' approach to language may work well for you, because by simply spending time with native speakers, or in the country of origin of your chosen language, your learning may appear to be random, but somehow it 'just happens'.

If you are a person who has a 'specific' pattern you will pay attention to detail. You will notice when a specific word is different when listening to a native. You will be more inclined to consciously pick up differences in grammar, because you can hear the detail. You will also be more inclined to take detailed notes of new words or other useful information.

We have outlined a few useful people types here - and there are many more. Recognising and understanding them will help you judge the usefulness of your particular traits and adapt your studying accordingly.

Now, to move this into the concept of culture, the concept of a continuum also applies to language and languages. People in different countries have different ways of being, and thus different cultures have different peculiarities, and these are reflected in the language and associated 'body language' (see Step Nineteen) of that culture.

> **CASE STUDY**
>
> **Motivation**
>
> A researcher called Stephen Krashen cites the story of L., a seventeen year old student in Israel. She already spoke some English with her parents at home, but her English writing was not good - she could not spell, her vocabulary was poor and her writing unintelligible. She had had tuition, and correcting her errors had failed miserably. Other corrective activities had resulted in short-term positive results, but no-long term improvement.
>
> Then, after a summer of no contact with her, her tutor set her an essay to write. The result was, he said: "…an almost perfect essay". Not only was the spelling good, but her expression was excellent and her vocabulary had improved beyond recognition. He discovered she had been reading all through the summer. She had been motivated to read in the language she was learning and had spent many hours in the library, enjoying books and magazines.

Key learning point from step four

- We are all different and understanding your individual motivational patterns will help you learn

Step Five
Understanding your personal learning style/s (1)
How to identify the ways in which you learn best: using your senses

We all learn differently. As a result, while 'experts' may suggest to you that there are specific 'best' ways to learn a language - often according to the latest research - not all methods suit all people. It is necessary for you to establish which learning styles suit you best, and incorporate which elements really work for you.

Note that learning styles are different from 'inhibitions'. If, for instance, you are embarrassed by talking to people using your new language skills, then it is necessary for you to overcome this embarrassment if you want to learn a language. This is not about your learning style, but is a learned inhibition which, in this instance, it is useful to change.

To learn most effectively we need to use all our senses. Learning activities that incorporate pictures, sounds, activity, and even taste and smell, will enhance speedy language acquisition.

However, we all have dominant senses. If you can learn which is your dominant sense (or sometimes two dominant senses) then you can concentrate most of your energy on activities using these senses and thus make learning easier for yourself. However, it's also important to improve those senses that you rely on less, so that you can expand your learning.

Most people's dominant senses are sight, activity or sound - and, of these, sight and activity are considered to be more common, at least in the Western world.

Here are some pointers to help you recognise your dominant sense/s

If you have a dominant **feeling** sense (touch and emotions), then the likelihood is that:

- You speak slowly and with feeling.
- You breathe low in your chest.
- You spend a lot of time looking down.
- You appreciate the texture of materials.
- When you remember events or situations you have been in, you are likely to remember the emotion associated with that event or situation.
- You will want to go out and try out your language skills - not just sit at home and learn from books.
- When you speak, you are likely to use body movements more because you are animated than to emphasise what you are saying.
- You don't like to sit still for long and are inclined to fidget if you are not able to move around.
- When giving directions, you will use lots of gestures and pointing.
- You are likely to use words such as: "It feels great" (an emotional phrase) or "I can handle this" (a tactile phrase).

If you have a dominant **visual** sense, then the likelihood is that:

- You will speak quite quickly.
- You will do a lot of looking up.
- Your breathing will be high in your chest.
- You will find it easy to visualise, and remember, something someone describes to you.
- You enjoy looking at graphs, charts, pictures and maps.
- You will 'see' words and sounds in your head.
- You may use your hands to aid a description you are presenting.
- When giving directions you would prefer to draw a diagram - and are likely to use words describing what the person will 'see'.
- You are likely to use words such as: "I see what you mean", or "It looks OK to me" ('visual' phrases).

If you have a dominant **hearing** sense, then the likelihood is that:

* You will have quite an even, rhythmic tone when you speak.
* Clarity of sound matters to you.
* Your breathing will be central to chest - and quite even.
* You may be quite slow answering questions as you are thinking them through in your head.
* You can remember the sound of someone saying a new word.
* You are likely to lean your head to one side or another when you are recalling sounds.
* Music resonates with you - and certain noises really grate on you.
* If you are giving instructions to someone you will be more likely to give them verbally and may well repeat them using sequential gestures; i.e using fingers to say: "First you do…, next you do…, then you do…etc."
* You are likely to use words such as: "That rings a bell with me" or to ask a question such as: "Do you hear what I'm saying?"

Understanding how your dominant sense relates to language learning

If you have a **feelings** dominance, you can improve your language learning by:

* Being aware of people's gestures and copying them.
* Walking around when you are memorising or learning things.
* Playing music that you love, quietly, in the background as you are learning or memorising - this will encourage feelings of well-being.
* Physically experiencing the language you are learning - becoming immersed in it.
* Creating activities for yourself to aid your learning by writing words down on a big poster or by putting new words on lots of bits of paper and sorting them.

If you have a **visual** dominance, you can improve your language learning by:

- Setting up pictures - and more pictures - to help you remember things.
- Writing the words associated with the pictures next to each picture in order to remember them.
- When you hear a new sound, creating a picture in your mind of what the sound looks like (either the actual words or a representation) and looking upwards and registering the picture for a few seconds.
- Writing down lists of words that will help you - keep a note book for this purpose.
- Drawing the words - or elements of a word - that are more difficult to remember in bright colours - or with big, or different letters:

If you have a **hearing** dominance, you can improve your language learning by:

- Playing lots of audio material - wherever you are, have your tapes, CDs, MP3 player etc with you.
- Creating tapes of words, phrases or elements that you want to learn and playing them over to yourself frequently. This is a useful learning tool because you can play them when you are doing the washing up, or cooking, or cleaning - or when you are at the bus stop, or in a train, or in a car.
- Consciously listening to what people are saying in your chosen language and repeating the words to yourself in your head.
- Listening to radio programmes in your chosen language.
- Getting involved in lots of discussions in your chosen language.

People with a hearing dominance have the edge when learning languages - and everyone can develop these skills.

Now you've found out about the ways in which you can use your senses, here are some useful activities you can do, which will fit in with your own personal preferences:

If you have a feelings preference

- If you are in the country where your chosen language is spoken, go to a public place and find a few people who look very different from you. Walk near them and, as you do, attempt to walk as they do, changing your posture accordingly. Imagine what may be going on in their heads as they are walking and imagine how they may be feeling. Notice whether your different posture and thought processes changes your own feelings (see 'Mirror Neurones' in Step Nineteen). If you are in your own country, you can go to a shopping centre and do the same exercise there with the people around you. And, wherever you do the exercise, make sure the people you are copying don't notice you doing so!

If you have a visual preference

- Acquire a short video/DVD of some people communicating in your chosen language (preferably two people, rather than a group, so the communication is kept fairly simple).
- Play the video with the sound turned down.
- Guess what subject the people are communicating about.
- Depending on how much you already know in that language, guess what they are actually saying.
- Turn up the volume and see how much you guessed correctly.

If you have a hearing preference

- Acquire a short audio tape/CD of two or more people communicating in your chosen language (again, if possible, keep it to two people for simplicity).
- Play the tape sentence by sentence, stopping it after each one.
- Turn off the tape. Turn on a blank tape and repeat what was said - recording it onto the new tape.
- Do this until you are at the end of the original audio tape.
- Compare them by running them both and listening to how similar or different they are.
- Repeat the exercise until you are satisfied that your effort is correct.

ACTIVITY

We have talked about the senses that we use, and explained that the main three senses are seeing, hearing and feeling (emotions and touch). We do, of course, use our smell and taste too and, for some people, they are particularly important - we know of one person for whom smell is the dominant sense. (And, interestingly, cooking the native dishes of a country associated with your chosen language, can help your learning experience, by giving you a stronger link to its culture.)

We are now going to tell you a story and, as you read it, become conscious of which of the senses you become most aware of and become 'real' for you. Be conscious, too, that your awareness may be either positive or negative (for example, we know someone who does not like the sensation of birds flying over her head, so imagining that happening would not be pleasant for her. However, the effect shows that one of her dominant senses is 'feeling' (the feeling of them flying overhead).

She was new to the country and it was an amazing pleasure for her to be able to put on her wind-proof coat, her Wellingtons, and her warm hat and gloves, and stride out into the elements. She walked up the garden path, over the gravel car park (those stones always felt odd under her feet) and turned right down the lane. On either side were new young stinging nettles just showing themselves in the hedgerow - she must remember, as they grew bigger, to avoid touching them.

The grass in the middle of the lane felt soft under her feet - Wellingtons really didn't have very thick soles. She could smell the hay that the farmer had put out for the sheep. She could also smell the fertilizer that he had been spreading too - it seemed to have a taste to it - almost medicinal.

As she walked, she became aware of so many sounds. The birds were very noisy. The Blackbird was loudest and most persistent, but there were softer, more melodic, sounds from other birds, too. And that rustling. She knew that was the silly Pheasants, who would suddenly fly out of the grass and, even though she expected it, never ceased to shock her.

She had turned left, climbed the hill (she was really breathing heavily) and was on the path going through the trees now. She popped a strong peppermint into her mouth - it always seemed to help when her mouth had dried from exertion. There was the old tree stump. The fairies live under there in the dark dank hollow and were responsible for the wild flowers (her grand-child loved this story)!

She experienced the comforting sound of twigs breaking as she walked across the dying branches, and the persistence of the bracken, which never failed to hit her as she walked through it, but which smelled so sweet. The wind in the trees continued to delight her - the movement as the canopies swayed and the soft whining as the sound echoed through the wood.

What was that? It was the sound of a scurrying creature scavenging for food; a mother taking precious bits to its nest where a bundle of tiny creatures lay in some dark hole, in their warm bed waiting for mum to return. Creatures that were completely dependent.

On the homeward path now, she emerged through the trees onto a little beach. Off came her shoes - she wanted to feel the sand between her toes. Oh, and the water was so very cold. The beach was small, on the edge of the fast-flowing river. The smells were different here - of water and fish and weeds. There was a Dipper bobbing up and down on a rock- the sun shining through the trees onto the wet rocks which shone brightly. It was so very peaceful.

She heard an anguished shout: "Come quickly, you are needed, urgently ……". Mood shattered, she ran.

Jot down which of the experiences in this story you remember most, and how you remembered them. Did you see pictures? Did you hear sounds? Was it an emotion you felt? Or did the smells and tastes pop into your mind?

Key learning points from step five

- People use different senses when communicating, thinking and learning
- Once you identify your own dominant sense/s you will be better able to create a study programme for yourself that really works for you
- Practising activities using your preferred senses will speed up your learning process
- Remember to explore the use of your least preferred sense - do something different

Step Six
Identifying your personal learning style/s (2)
How to recognise factors that may affect your learning: 'intelligences'

As well as dominant senses, which were discussed in Step Five, we also have dominant intelligences. It was Professor Howard Gardner of Harvard University who identified that we, as humans, are not just 'intelligent' but that we have lots of different ways of being intelligent. Traditionally we were considered to be intelligent if we were able to understand our native language and if we could work with numbers.

Gardner described eight intelligences and, following his theories, others have been recognised. The following section covers a number of intelligences and gives you suggestions for learning activities that work best for people who are dominant in each particular intelligence.

Look through the categories that follow and identify the ones that seem to describe you best. When you know what is your dominant intelligence (and of course you may have more than one), you will be able to select those activities that will speed up your learning. And, as with your senses, the ideal is to develop those intelligences that are under-developed, so that you can use them all.

Here are some 'intelligent' activities:

Linguistic intelligence

With this intelligence you are likely to be able to pick up the meaning of words, to pick up their rhythms and their sounds - very useful for language learning.

Useful activities would be to:

- Listen to native speakers without speaking and guess, through their body language, and what they say, what they are communicating.

- Spend some time mimicking someone who speaks in your chosen language.

Logical/mathematical intelligence

With this intelligence you are likely to be a good problem solver, and like order, and sequence - and perceive patterns easily.

Useful activities would be to:

- Have a look at the research on the development of language - particularly in children - because it will make your language learning more interesting to you.
- Look for patterns when you are learning, or repeating, new words and phrases. What is similar? What is repeated? Write down what you are learning in a logical order - an order that seems rational to you.

Visual/spatial intelligence

With this intelligence, the same features apply as if you have a dominant visual sense - so similar activities would be appropriate.

Useful activities would be to:

- Create large images of the words you are learning, coloured in primary colours, and put them high on your walls - consciously look at the words frequently.
- Create a flow chart of your language learning. What have you done so far? What have you learned so far? What do you intend to do next? What will you do in the long term? Change the colours, or put stars or markers, when you have achieved something.

Bodily/kinaesthetic intelligence

With this intelligence, it is the same as having a dominant kinaesthetic sense and, again, similar activities apply. For all learners, however, physical movement aids learning.

Useful activities would be to:

- Watch a video of two native speakers conversing and consciously notice what they 'do' rather than what they 'say'.
- Spend more time with native speakers than at home with your books!
- Get together with one or more other people who are learning the same language Then you, together with one other person, create a scenario - in the chosen language - for the others to interpret. Enjoy it if anyone is able to correct any language you have used.
- Use 'Brain Gym' to develop co-ordination and balance and to put you into a good learning state (see Appendix).

Musical intelligence

Many people learn through their natural ability to assimilate music. Young learners learn through being aware of accent, tempo and rhythm. Emulate them!

Useful activities would be to:

- Learn songs in your chosen language.
- Read, and recite, poems in your chosen language.
- When you are learning phrases, beat out a rhythm as you say them.
- Listen for the musical cadences in the chosen language - and copy them.

Interpersonal intelligence

With this intelligence, you are likely to enjoy being with other people and interacting with them. If you know you are good at this then, because this intelligence is so fundamental to learning second languages, you are already ahead of the game with your learning.

Useful activities would be to:

- Create situations, whereby you are listening to others in your chosen language, and acting on what you have heard.

- Go to a place where there are people who speak in your chosen language, and start up a casual conversation with someone - 'passing the time of day'.

Intrapersonal intelligence

With this intelligence you are likely to enjoy doing things on your own and understanding yourself - what a useful intelligence. You are likely to be self-motivated and are likely to have a keen knowledge of what is important to you.

Useful activities would be to:

- Notice, as you communicate with native speakers, how you feel about doing this, and adjust your situation until you feel comfortable. For instance, choose to talk to a child if you are embarrassed talking to an adult.

- Reflect on, and analyse, what learning is useful to you and what is less useful. Exchange ideas and hints and tips.

Naturalist intelligence

With this intelligence, you are sensitive to the natural environment.

Useful activities would be to:

- Learn words and phrases that are associated with nature.

- Go out walking and, as you do so, create a story about your physical environment and tell it to yourself in your chosen language.

- Learn words and phrases that are associated with nature and the seasons.

ACTIVITY
Assessing your dominant intelligences
Simply take the intelligences that we have mentioned in this section and give each of them a ranking out of ten. One means that you believe you use that intelligence very little and ten means that you use it very much Once you have gone through all of them, you should end up with a ranking that shows you which are probably your most dominant intelligencies. You can use this information to consider which learning processes are likely to work best for you.

Key learning points from Step Six

- People are intelligent in different ways
- By identifying your own dominant intelligences you can help yourself create a study programme that works for you
- Using activities that fit with your dominant intelligences will help you learn more speedily
- You can develop your intelligences

Section Two
Study skills
The skills you need to improve your ability to learn

This part of the book will give you key tips for making sure that your studies work for you.

We will be covering the following:
- Setting goals.
- Choosing the best times to study.
- Deciding where to study.
- Reading effectively.
- Taking effective notes.
- Using your memory effectively.
- Using aids to learning.
- Creating a learning log.

Step Seven
Setting goals

You already have your overall purpose for your studies, which is important, but this needs to be re-enforced by shorter-term goals. These short-term goals will keep you focussed on what you want to achieve, keep you on track, give you ways of assessing your progress and help motivate you as you achieve each one in turn and produce results.

Goals need to have a number of qualities; important ones are:

- To be specific - so that you can say exactly what it is you want to achieve.
- To have an associated time-frame - so you know when you want to have achieved your goal by.
- To be measurable - so you can tell when you have achieved your goal.
- To have 'standards' attached to them - so you know what level of proficiency you are aiming for.
- To be achievable - so that you know it's possible for you to get the results you want.

There are many kinds of goal you can set for yourself; here are some examples:

Quantity

- How many hours of formal study you would like to do in a week.
- How many words you would like to learn in a week.
- What proportion of your total studying you would like to achieve in a three-month period.

Quality

- Being able to have a mutually understandable conversation with a friend in your chosen language.
- Being able to understand a foreign language film without looking at the sub-titles.
- Being able to read a particular book in its original language.

EXERCISE

Goal setting

- Pick three things you would like to achieve from your language studies.

- Write them down.

- Add time-scales to each one.

- Now, look at the three things and check that you have made your goals sufficiently specific. For example, if you said you would like to be able to read in your chosen language, being specific would mean saying you would like to be able to read a newspaper, a letter from a friend, a technical book or an email from a work colleague; just saying 'reading' would be too general.

- Make sure you specify the standard you wish to achieve in each goal, (for example being able to speak words with an authentic native accent is a higher standard than simply being able to speak the words with an English accent).

- And make sure that your goals are actually achievable by you personally. If you have a time-scale of one month and you want to have the ability to read technical reports within that time, while fitting in your studies very part-time, you might find it too much of a stretch - so do check that you put realistic things down on your list.

Key learning points from step seven

Goals need to have qualities:

- Be specific
- Be time-related
- Be measurable
- Be achievable
- Have standards associated with them

Step Eight
Going at your own pace and studying when it's best for you

When you learn something new, it's important to go at a pace that's right for you. When you go to a class, there's likely to be a set timetable that everyone has to fit in with. It's at a specific time of day and for a specific length of time, and you have to work through, regardless of how you feel, how busy your day has been, how much energy you have and how much you are able to concentrate.

When your learning is self-directed - which means that you are in control of what you learn and when you learn it - you are much better able to work at your own pace, go over things as often as you need, and fit your learning into your own way of life.

There are two key things to think about here:
• Your lifestyle.
• Your 'body clock'.

When you decide to learn a language, it takes a commitment in terms of both time and energy. You need to consider both of these if you are really going to achieve the results you want. Your lifestyle will influence the time you spend on learning and your 'body clock' will influence the energy you have for it, so let's look at each of these in turn:

Your lifestyle

You will learn best when your studying fits in with the rest of your life. This means you should consider what else you have to do, so you can find out how to fit in your learning in the best way possible. Some of the things you might like to take into account are:

Your family

What family activities do you need to work around? Do you have a young baby that needs regular feeds? Do you have children that have to be taken to and from school at particular times? Do you have to cook an evening meal for yourself and your family? Do you have elderly relatives you have to visit on a daily or weekly basis?

Your work commitments

Do you have a regular job that takes up much of each weekday? Do you work shifts so that certain times of day are always committed? Do you travel on business so you are away from home a lot? Do you have a high-pressure job that requires long hours and complete concentration?

Your other activities

Do you have lots of social activities? Do you do charity work? Do you have animals to look after? Do you have lots of weekends away? Do you have a time-consuming hobby?

Each of these areas will make demands on your time and need to be taken into account when working out how you will study. So have a go at the following exercise to help you plan your time.

EXERCISE
Time planning

Take a sheet of paper and write down the main things you need to spend time on. It helps to break down the main categories we've already mentioned - family, work and other activities - into smaller ones for this purpose. For example: travelling, gardening, cleaning, cooking and eating, working, watching TV, visiting friends and so on. Remember to include time for sleeping, rest, exercise and relaxation too.

There are two ways of writing down these areas; the first is simply to make a list and the second is drawing a 'Mind Map®'. A Mind Map® is a diagram, created by Tony Buzan, who has written many books on this subject. If you go to Step Eleven you will see an example of a Mind Map® diagram and, if you find this more helpful than simply making a list, you can put your own activities down in this way, having spaces for whichever activities are most important in your own life.

When you have each activity down, you can give it a time allocation - in other words how many hours a day you spend on this activity and which days of the week it has to be done on. You can then see what time you have left for your studying. And it may be that, because of your own calendar, your studying has to be done on specific days of the week - doing this exercise will help you work this out.

If you find that your calendar is so full that there seems to be no time at all left for studying, you will need to make time. This means you will have to give up something else in order to study. Maybe you can 'delegate' something to someone else while you study - for example can someone else take the dog for a walk or collect your child from school. Alternatively, can you get up half an hour earlier to make more time in your day? When you are determined to succeed, there is always a way of making it happen.

Now let's look at the second area:

Your body-clock

Everyone has an internal 'clock'. You may have noticed this when you had to get up at a particular time one morning and, although you set an alarm clock, you actually woke up at that time anyway - just before the clock went off.

Our body clocks also control our energy levels. Some people are called 'Owls' because they have lots of energy late in the evening; others are called 'Larks' because they have most energy early in the morning. And there's a difference between physical and mental energy. Research shows that we all have times when we are most mentally alert and other times when we are most capable of physical exertion.

Because of this, when you are learning something new, it helps to understand your own energy levels so that you can fit in your studying at the most beneficial times for you. People sometimes fail to learn, not because they aren't capable, but simply because are studying at the wrong time of day for them personally.

Here's an exercise to find out your best times for studying.

EXERCISE
Working out your own energy levels

Take a large sheet of paper and mark it as the diagram here shows - a column for each day of the week and a horizontal line for each fifteen-minute period during the day.

	SUN	MON	TUES	WED	THUR	FRI	SAT
9.00 - 9.15 AM		M 5 P 1	M 5 P 1				
9.15 - 9.30 AM		M 5 P 2	M 5 P 1				
9.30 - 9.45 AM		M 5 P 3	M 4 P 2				
9.45 - 10.00 AM		M 4 P 3	M 4 P 2				

15 MINUTE INTERVALS

Keep your diary for a few days (a week if possible) and, in each box, write a letter M and a letter P. The M stands for mental energy and the P stands for physical energy. It's good to use a different colour pen for each of these letters. Leave space for a number against each letter and, at the end of each fifteen-minute period, write a number against the M and another number against the P. If you had a very high energy level write in a 5, for a reasonably high level write in a 4, for an average level write a 3, for a low level write a 2 and for a very low energy level write a 1.

At the end of the week you will be able to look back and see when your best times were for high mental and physical energy. Studying is best when your energy levels are high, so plan your future studying for times that work best for you. If you are most alert in the evenings, study then; if you are best late morning, study then. If your other commitments absolutely prevent you from studying at your best times, just be aware that you will need to get yourself into a good frame of mind for learning and the exercises on the accompanying CD will help you do this.

Key learning points from step eight

- If you have a very full diary, you will have to make time to study
- Keeping a diary of what you do for a few days helps you work out when to fit in your studying
- You have an internal 'body-clock' that allows you to function best at certain times of day
- You can work out which times of day are best for you to study - these will be the times when your learning is likely to be most effective
- Studying when you are mentally and physically alert will give you the best results

Step Nine
Deciding where you will study

You know *when* is best for you to study; you have planned your study time. But where will you study? This, you may think, is a silly question. At a table? At your desk? In the kitchen? In front of the telly? (We are not discussing your going out to find native speakers here, because you will do that whenever you can).

Don't be mistaken - if you are serious about your study then you need to associate a particular place with serious learning.

Have you noticed that when you walk into the kitchen you think of food? Have you noticed that when you walk into the bedroom you either imagine the bliss of being cuddled up in your bed, or else you think of getting yourself dressed up (if you have your clothes in there). Have you noticed that the main room in your house, where people congregate - is where you feel you want to socialise? And if you go out to work, when you get there you adopt a different mind set - because you are in your 'place of work'. This process of associating a feeling with a location or event is called *'anchoring'* and you can choose to make it work for you.

So, for studying, decide on a place where you will be reading language books, or looking up vocabulary, or reading this book - whatever you are doing to help you learn the language you are so keen to learn. That place might be in your bedroom, it might be at a table in the social room (only be aware that you might get distracted), or it could be a space under the stairs.

Wherever it is, make it your own - make it the place that, when you go there, you are in the mind-set to do your language learning. And of course it is a place where you can leave your books and notes, which means you don't have to keep tidying away your books, forgetting which one you were looking at, or losing your place in something you are reading.

Do this and your unconscious mind will know that you are serious about learning that new language.

The second advantage of this special space of yours is that here you can collect together all the resources you need. When they are in one place, and easily accessible, you are more likely to return to your learning - everything will be there; you won't have to search round for your books, or notes, or coloured pens. Ideally have them near to where your computer is (more of that later).

If you have the space, put up pictures of the country whose language you are learning and put up lots of new words in big colourful letters - maybe a new word to learn every day. Make your space interesting and colourful and somewhere you want to return to.

TIP

If you are struggling with a problem - maybe not understanding some words, or being unable to find some information it can be useful to stay in your study space until you have solved the problem. And changing your posture may help, as may looking up. Otherwise, if you say to yourself: "I'll look for that tomorrow", your unconscious mind will associate tomorrow's study with having to do something you were struggling with and you are less likely to want to return. Sort the problem, feel the sense of achievement, and know that next time you return you will be doing something new, interesting and exciting. However, if you really can't sort out the problem, don't force yourself to keep going - you should use your own judgment about when it's best to call it a day and perhaps go for a walk or sleep on the problem - sometimes just doing something different helps you to sort things out.

Key learning points from step nine
- Have your own learning space to return to
- Preferably, don't leave an unsolved problem at the end of a learning session

Step Ten
Reading Effectively

Reading with a purpose means that you **decide in advance of anything you read why you are reading it.** Are you reading to understand the origin of a language? Are you reading to learn new vocabulary? Are you reading to get a more general idea of the culture of the people who speak your chosen language? Are you reading to improve your ability to speak a language?

A researcher called William Perry did some very profound research many years ago, from which he discovered that we have some exceptionally capable readers in the West. However, these capable readers do not achieve very much. The conclusions from his research were that, in order to be effective, we need to read with a purpose.

Once you have a purpose you will be more effective. Once you have a purpose you will be able to choose the approach that you adopt.

Different purposes require different approaches; here are a few of them:

* If you want to learn new vocabulary - read new words, write them down, find out what they mean and write down their meanings.
* If you want to find out more about the origin of the language then read to understand - be fascinated.
* If you want to find out more about the culture, be aware of what you are looking for - question what, in the text you are reading, is giving you the insights into that culture.
* If you are reading to improve your ability to understand and speak the language then read whatever you choose, having first decided that this will be a helpful activity and that it is going to be interesting and fun reading something in your chosen language.

Once you have your purpose and start reading, here are a few tips to help you read effectively:

- Read in a good light - this will help you focus and prevent eye-strain.

- Make sure your posture is good and you have a comfortable seat.

- If you have any reading difficulties in your own language, experiment with using sheets of coloured plastic that you can place over the pages you are reading from. Research shows that many people improve their reading and concentration ability greatly when they do this. Because different colours work best for different people, you need to experiment with this - maybe pink is best for you, or perhaps yellow, or green, blue or some other colour. You can get coloured sheets in good stationery shops.

And the most important thing to remember is to really enjoy your reading.

ACTIVITY

- Find a topic that interests you - maybe an existing hobby.
- Read around the subject in your chosen language - find as much information as you can.
- Write an 'essay' on what you have learned. Just write - don't worry about getting the spelling or grammar correct. Let what you have to say 'flow'. Simply enjoy writing about a special interest, in another language.
- Read out loud, just to yourself or to a native speaker. This uses a different part of the brain from reading to yourself in your head.
- Get a native speaker to 'correct' what you have written, or get out some books and look up any words and phrases that you were not sure about - enjoy noticing how much you got correct.
- Talk to the native speaker about what you have learned from your reading.
- Apply the spelling strategy (See Step Eighteen) to the words you didn't quite get right.

Key learning points from step ten
- Read with a purpose
- Read as much as possible
- Make reading easy for yourself - good light, comfortable environment
- Read out aloud in your chosen language

Step Eleven
Listing words and taking effective notes

When you are learning a new language you will inevitably need to write down things that you have learned. We will cover two of these in this section.

1 Lists of new words

One of the main things you will need is a list of new words. Leonardo Da Vinci, when he taught himself Latin, simply produced a Lexicon (list of words) for himself. He was so passionate about words that this was a really exciting activity for him.

But lists of words, out of context, are really not much use. You need to make your notes interesting - and contextual.

So, remembering your own learning styles, what could you do to make your notes interesting? Here are some ideas for you:

* Just write down new words as you come across them (remember to have your dictionary nearby) - and you may choose to add the translation of each word.

* Write each new word in a sentence, highlighting the word that interests you.

* Produce a picture of what the word represents, with the word written underneath the picture.

* Record the new words - either individual words or sentences, or both, with or without translations.

* Create a collage of pictures of all the new words.

* Using bright colours, create a collage of brightly coloured words that you have learned.

* Create a 'teaching' book with the new words in - maybe with another learner in mind.

2 Other notes

There will be lots of other reasons to take notes, and these can be made in traditional style with headings and sub-headings in linear form.

However, you may choose to try Mind Maps® which we mentioned briefly earlier. Tony Buzan showed that the way in which the brain functions is not linear.

He devised a method of producing notes which was based on the concept that we have central thoughts that radiate out from our minds in no particular order. He was one of the first people to recognize that our minds make connections. Using key words and visual images, we can remember large amounts of information by connecting one image, or key word, to another.

Mind Maps® are 'organic'; they work best for most people when they are in full colour (at least three colours) and have lots of pictures.

The diagram below is an example of a Mind Map® but, to be useful, each of your Mind Maps® needs to be produced by you, for you, because they are a product of the connections that your mind makes.

The main value of Mind Maps® is in noting large amounts of information. They are excellent for brainstorming ideas too, and they are also good for planning (you may choose to produce one to plan your language-learning study). They are also good for remembering, especially if you are good at visualising, and we will be covering some memory techniques later.

An example of a Mind Map®:

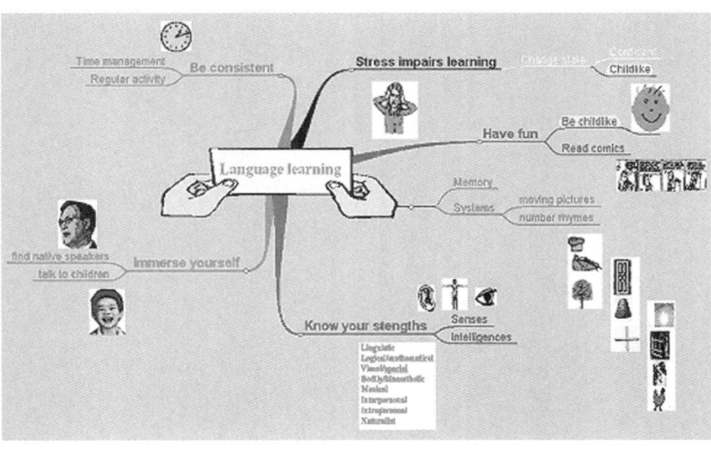

Key learning points from step eleven

- Make your lists of words interesting
- If you like linear notes, remember to use sub-headings and bullet-points and to emphasise words so they stand out
- Mind Maps® may work for you

Step Twelve
Using your memory effectively

We have talked about how your mind works, including how it attempts to make sense (sometimes out of nonsense) and how it makes connections.

The part of the brain that deals mostly with memory is called the Hippocampus. This is situated in the 'middle brain' (the 'mammalian' brain). That part of the brain is particularly associated with our emotions. Thus, memory and emotions are very closely associated.

Do you remember a time when you heard a piece of music and your mind was transported back to a situation in which you heard the music. Perhaps a picture of that time pops up into your mind.

The reason that situation popped up was because of the connection between your emotions and your memory - the situation you remembered was probably quite an emotional one - maybe good or maybe not so good. This is why, as we mentioned when discussing being in a good state, you are likely to remember more when you are feeling really great.

Another function of the same part of the brain is your imagination - when you create images in your mind that particular part of the brain is activated.

Your memory *and* your imagination use *the* same neurological circuits.

Types of memory

We have three main types of memory, which have various purposes:

Semantic Memory

The first type of memory is called **Semantic Memory**. (Semantics means the study of meaning in language). Semantic memory is a record of facts, skills and concepts that we have acquired in our lives - hence the need for a form of structure, such as mnemonics (using the first letters of a sequence of words, to aid memorisation) in order to recall them.

You may well remember the mnemonics you were taught when you were a child; for example '**R**ead **O**ut **Y**our **G**reen **B**ook **I**n **V**erse' for remembering the colours of the rainbow in sequence (**R**ed, **O**range, **Y**ellow, **G**reen, **B**lue, **I**ndigo, **V**iolet).

Using mnemonics to remember is always valuable and you may choose to create some for yourself in order to remember elements of grammar.

Semantic memory can also be recalled through using rhymes - which is why singing songs, or reciting little poems in your chosen language, is such an easy way to learn.

> *Find every opportunity you can to learn songs and poems in your chosen language - you might even learn advertising jingles too!*

Procedural Memory

The second type of memory is called **Procedural Memory**. This type of memory is not easy to describe. It's the memory that is stored in your body - the memory of how to walk, or how to ride a bike. Your body stores the memory of all the physical skills you have acquired in your life. Most of these skills are acquired through practice - laying down a path in your brain that results in long term memory.

For example, imagine that you look out of the window and there is thick snow outside. You put on your boots and warm clothes and go out and walk through the snow, leaving footprints. When you return to your house you leave more footprints - and it is quite likely that they are on top of the first ones. You are starting to lay down a pathway. Someone else in the house decides to go out too and, as it is easy to walk along the pathway you have already started, that pathway is now becoming more defined. On his or her return she chooses the same path - now it really is trodden down and looks like a path which any caller can use.

The more you return to that pathway the more permanent it becomes. So it is in your brain. The more you practise any activity, the more your brain remembers it and puts it into long-term memory. This is particularly true of activities, but is also true of the words you learn.

Episodic Memory

The third type of memory is **Episodic Memory**. We remember things in context. This is why, for most people, learning lists of vocabulary doesn't work. We need to learn words in context. Thus you can increase your learning ten-fold by immersing yourself in a culture - taking every opportunity you can to be with native speakers.

This is particularly relevant to the learning of grammar. The experts have very strong views on this. The consensus is that the brain is good at learning grammar, but poor at being taught it.

Stephen Pinker, an eminent researcher on language acquisition, maintains that language is a human instinct and that all societies have complex language structures, but that by using a language we will learn its grammatical rules without conscious effort.

Stephen Krashen feels very strongly about this and said: "Language is learned by focusing on the message, not the form". He commented:

"The research community has devoted an extraordinary amount of energy in an attempt to show that grammar teaching works. Instead, they have shown only what many, many language students have always realised: formal grammar instruction has a very limited impact upon second-language competence. Even intensive, prolonged instruction that is limited to just a few aspects of grammar results, in general, in only modest gains on tests in which students are encouraged to think about form".

Explorations in Language Acquisition and Use: The Taipei Lectures
Stephen D Krashen, Heinemann 2003 p.vii

So, you can choose between grammar drills, doing grammar exercises, being 'taught' grammar by rote - or you can play.

EXAMPLE

Michel Thomas (1914-2005) was an amazing linguist born in Poland. His fluency in several languages saved his life during the Second World War and he was an expert in using non-verbal communication. (He was also a good dog handler which seems to relate to use of non-verbal communication.)

Thomas set up a language school in Los Angeles and many film stars and politicians came there, including Grace Kelly, Emma Thompson and - more recently - the British comedian Eddie Izzard. Thomas discovered a way to teach languages so that learners could have fluency in both spoken and written language after three days with him and two days with an assistant. His approach to learning was that it was the teacher's responsibility to teach the language; the student had simply to stay in a good relaxed state, listen and repeat the carefully constructed programme that starts off by finding the language's similarities to English. In the process, students absorb, rather than learn by rote, the grammar of the language and some of the culture and beliefs of the native speakers.

In 1990 he made his programmes in French, German, Spanish and Italian available to the general public on tape and CD and, in 1997, BBC 2 televised a programme on Thomas's work. In the programme was a piece about an experiment to teach French to a group of teenagers, from a North London sixth-form college, who had previously failed at learning a language. With Thomas's approach, including changes to the environment, such as armchairs, curtains and good lighting, the teenagers made excellent progress in a short space of time.

A useful memory technique

Your brain needs structure. It likes to have previous experience to hook on to. It likes systems (such as mnemonics). In order to improve your memory, then, you can create structures to help your brain.

There are various systems that people have used over the years to help with memory, many dating back for centuries, and one very useful approach is number-rhyming systems. This kind of system is extremely helpful in remembering lists of items and can be extended to remembering a sequence of words when learning a second language.

The process works by taking a series of numbers, giving each number an associated word that rhymes with it, and then creating a picture (or it could be a sound) for each of the words. You then associate the picture with a second word, so linking them in your memory. Let's see how it works out in practice by taking the numbers from one to ten and associating each with a word that rhymes with them, as follows:

1 Bun

2 Shoe

3 Tree

4 Drawer

5 Hive

6 Sticks

7 Heaven

8 Weight

9 Vine

10 Hen

The next step is to memorise this list. It helps to create pictures to associate with each of the numbers. For number one (bun), for instance, you might create a picture of a big bun. For two (shoe) you might create a picture of a shoe that is attractive to you - maybe bright red so it stands out well. For three (tree) you might create a picture of a large tree with lots of shiny leaves.

Continue in this way until you have covered all ten numbers. If you don't wish to create pictures, then you can simply use the sound of the rhyme as a way of remembering the numbers.

If, however, you can produce a picture for each one it will probably help you most, because the mind remembers pictures better than anything - and in particular it remembers pictures that are large, ridiculous or sexy!

For the sake of understanding this technique, let's decide we want to remember the German numbers from one to ten, although you don't have to use the technique to remember numbers - it's very effective for any sequence of other words, such as a shopping list, parts of a car or items in a recipe.

So, going back to the German numbers, first we have to create something that is familiar from these unfamiliar words. Here are some suggestions.

Remember that getting your pronunciation right is more important than getting the spelling right at this stage, so concentrate on the sounds in the brackets rather than the original words themselves.

German numbers from one to ten

Eins (eyns) - a picture of ice with a big N in the middle.

Zwei (tsvigh) - a couple of snakes intertwined vying for position and making a sssss noise as they do.

Drei (dry) - speaks for itself - a picture of something very dry.

Vier (feer) - fear (a picture of a cartoon head with hair standing on end).

Fünf (fuenf) - someone collapsing on a cushion; the sound it makes is 'fuenf'.

Sechs (zeks) - sacks - maybe plastic bin-liners.

Sieben (zee-bin) - 'I am looking in zee bin'.

Acht (akht) - a theatre stage with someone doing a comedy act.

Neun (noin) - a person with a Birmingham accent saying it is 'nine' (o'clock).

Zehn (tsane) - a picture of the left bank of the river in Paris - the river Seine.

In order to remember these as numbers, they need to be associated with the number rhyming system. So now combine the two pictures:

1 Bun - Eins (eyns) - Combine the ice with the bun - say have a big bun with ice dripping off it with the big N as the decoration in the middle.

2 Shoe - Zwei (tsvigh) - Combine the snakes with the shoe - say have each snake sitting in a shoe.

3 Tree - Drei (dry) - Combine the tree with something dry - say a tree which has leaves that are dry and crisp and hanging from the branches.

4 Drawer - Vier (feer) - Combine a drawer with something to do with fear - say a cartoon head, with hair standing on end, peering into a drawer.

5 Hive - Funf (fuenf) - Combine the cushion with a hive - say a bee hive behind the cushion, where all the bees are disturbed by the noise and are flying up and around in anger.

6 Sticks - Sechs (zeks) - Combine sticks with sacks - say large sacks containing sticks for firewood.

7 Heaven - Sieben (zee-bin) - Combine a bin with heaven - say a cartoon character looking in 'zee bin' with a balloon shape coming from his head and picturing a heavenly image (maybe what he hopes to find when he looks in 'zee- bin') - the more ridiculous the image is, the better you will remember it.

8 Weight - Acht (akht) - Combine the actor with a weight - say a pantomime dame lifting a weight.

9 Vine - Neun (noin) - Combine the person with the accent and a vine - say the person has a grapevine draped around the head - with nine grapes on it.

10 Hen - Zehn (tsane) - Combine the river with a hen - say a giant hen drinking from the water in the river.

This may appear, on paper, to be a very complicated process. However, having created some images - and it is much better if you create images of your own - we can just about *guarantee* that you will remember the images and the associated numbers - and thus the new words that you want to remember.

Take time to create the systems that your mind will use.

ACTIVITY
Remembering words

1) Make a list of 'objects' you would like to identify in your chosen language.

2) Connect to the Internet and go to Google or another search engine. Click on 'images'.

3) Type in the English word for each object and find an appropriate picture which represents the object.

4) Download the picture and place it on a page (as large as possible), then type its description in your chosen language beneath the picture. Print the picture. If you are learning a 'picture' language such as Chinese, print the picture first and then write its description beneath the picture.

5) Put the pictures where you will see them regularly and move them around from time to time so they don't become so 'familiar' that you stop noticing them.

By only putting the chosen language description below each picture, rather than the English plus the chosen language descriptions, you are directly associating each object with its description in the language you wish to learn.

As a final point to this section, if you are concerned about how much you will be able to remember because of your age, it's important to understand that, if you exercise your mind, you will be able to keep your memory active and even improve it. Just like training the muscles of your body, training your mind will be enormously helpful in your learning activities.

Key learning points from step twelve

- Memory and emotions are associated
- Use mnemonics
- The brain lays down pathways
- Learning in context is easy
- Your brain needs structure and systems for understanding

Step Thirteen
Using aids to learning

We have already talked about many aids to learning - pictures, tapes, books and people. Now we can include technological aids to help you learn well.

These include:

- Television.
- Radio.
- Mobile music players (MP3 Players/Ipods).
- Video/DVD and other formats.
- Your computer and the Internet.
- 'Music to learn by'.

Television

Chat shows, soap operas, quiz shows and reality TV programmes are a great source of content for learning in your chosen language - they are usually high in emotion, which is helpful in language learning. And you can check for non-verbal communication with the sound turned down.

Radio

This is a good source of material to improve your listening and comprehension in your chosen language. We have met many people who learnt English just by listening to the World Service programmes - without ever visiting an English-speaking country.

Portable audio-players - CD/MP3 players/ ipods, etc

Language courses that come in multi-disc formats can be downloaded for personal use onto a tiny piece of equipment making it easy to carry around and use at your convenience - indoors or out. And you can use ear-phones with them, but please make sure that they can't be heard by other people - hissy, indistinguishable sounds can be very annoying to others.

Video (VHS, DVD and other formats that may appear)

These are all useful and some give you options to view video material with or without sub-titles and in different languages. It is possible to get a product that has material you can watch first in your native language, so that you understand its content, and then in your chosen language, to enhance your learning.

Computers

You can easily learn a language without the aid of a computer. However, it may be that language-learning can lead you to learning about computers - a good cross-fertilization. And even if you don't own a computer you may be able to use one at your local library.

In 1965, George Moore, of the computer-chip manufacturer Intel, predicted that computer technology would double about every 18 months. This has proved very accurate and no doubt the pace will continue, or increase, from now on.

Your computer and the Internet
Are you aware that your computer is an amazing resource?

Software

- That you can get software to enable your computer to read out what is written on a page on your screen?

- That software enables you to type a sentence into your computer in one language and have it translated, automatically, into another language.

- That you can create exciting, interesting and stimulating pictures - and words - on your computer, print them and put them where you can see them regularly in order to aid your learning.

The Internet

- That you can find web-sites that are written in just about every language in the world - good for reading practice.

- That using the new technology, such as MP3 or podcasts, you can download many pieces of sound, in many languages, on numerous subjects to your computer or MP3 player.

- That if you have email, you can easily get yourself an Internet pen-pal in your chosen language and exchange written conversations.

- That if you have Internet connection, through 'Instant Messenger' you can write, in real-time, to people in other countries.

- That through Skype (or other similar telephonic connections) you can talk to people in other countries - at no cost at all other than your Internet connection.

- That there are many interest groups you can join and contribute to that discuss your favourite subject - and not just in English.

- That you can find a lot of information about the culture of the country of your target language; the more you know about the culture, the more you are likely to understand the language.

- That there is lots of free information on learning your chosen language - all you have to do is search for it.

Health warning
Manage your state at the computer or TV screen

It is very easy to:

- Let time drift by while you are watching a screen.

- Slump.

- Sit in one position for hours on end.

- Stop breathing regularly, or blinking, as you get absorbed.

To rectify these things you can:

- Sit in an upright position where possible.

- Put a note, like a Post-It® on the corner of your computer with the words 'breathe' and 'blink' on it.

- Look away from the screen every 20 minutes (and more frequently if possible).

Music to learn by

Our brains work best when they are functioning in a particular way. Bulgarian psychiatrist and teacher, Georgi Lozanov, born in 1926, was founder of the Suggestopaedia language learning method. He advocated using different kinds of music to evoke different learning states in students.

Where appropriate, the teacher's voice works in rhythm with the music to enhance learning and relaxation. Sometimes the music is more energising than relaxing. Lozanov's method is sometimes called Accelerated Learning in Europe and America.

There are specific brain 'rhythms' that enhance learning. In particular, the 'Alpha Brain Rhythms' assist relaxation and suggestion.

You can use music to help your brain achieve these rhythms and thereby increase your learning ability. The music that seems to work best for this purpose is Baroque music (c1600-1750), which has a fluid structure and plays at 8-12 cycles per second or 60 beats a minute. The heart-rate tends to synchronise with the beat of the music and so affect the brain rhythms.

You will be able to find many recordings of this kind and you may like to experiment with using them while you are studying, or while you are visualising, in order to improve your learning.

Key learning points from step thirteen

- Technology can aid your learning
- The Internet is an unlimited source of learning material
- Be aware of your posture and eyes when spending time at your computer

Step Fourteen
Keeping a learning log

Records of progress

A very useful aid to your studies is keeping a record of what you have done and how you have progressed. There are a number of benefits to doing this:

- You can see how far you have gone to achieving the results you want.
- You can see how much you have left to do.
- You can keep notes on what you have done.
- You can record your thoughts on your progress.
- You can consider those things you enjoy, or do well.
- You can consider those things you don't enjoy or don't feel you do as well.
- You can record ideas you have.
- You can record useful things you have come across (for example tips and strategies for learning).
- You can make notes of things you wish to do next.

A learning log can be designed exactly as you wish - here are some suggestions for what you can allow space for:

- Listing goals and progress towards them.
- Writing thoughts and ideas.
- Pasting in useful pieces of information.
- Adding vocabulary.

You can also consider whether you prefer your learning log to be mainly textual, linear and structured (eg lists and columns) or mainly diagrammatic and organic (eg Mind Maps® - see earlier sections). Which of these you prefer depends on your own motivational and learning styles - a logical learner (see Step Six) will prefer structure and order; someone who is dyslexic may prefer a more fluid way of mapping their progress.

If you like using Mind Maps®, you can use them to create learning plans for yourself and to show what you have actually learned.

Another thing that you can do on your computer is keep a web-diary in your chosen language

Many people are keeping web-page logs (blogs) on the Internet. This growing phenomenon is essentially an online diary. Blogs are generally a place to follow the lives of people you've never heard of and to gain insight into what's on the mind of people from other countries.

At the time of writing:

9% of Internet users say they have created blogs.

6% of the entire U.S. adult population have created blogs. (That's almost one out of every 20 people, or approximately 11 million American adults.)

And people do read them. In fact, 1 in 6 adults (and 1 in 4 Internet users) areblog readers - that's nearly 20% of newspaper readers and almost 40% of talk radio listeners. And people will comment on your blog, or link to it, or email you or just read it.

Since Blogger was launched in 2001, blogs have reshaped the web, impacted politics, shaken up journalism, and enabled millions of people to connect with others.

Key learning points from step fourteen

- Keeping a learning log helps you to monitor your progress
- Writing a blog can provide support for you from others

Step Fifteen
Assessing your learning

Although we have given this a new section heading, you will already have considered assessment when creating a learning log for yourself. However, while a learning log is more of an ongoing learning aid, true assessment is an important stage in your learning strategy.

Assessment should be built in to your study programme and can be carried out at various stages:

- At the 'end' of your total programme (if there is a formal end to it).
- At the end of each 'stage' of your learning.
- At the end of each specific learning activity.

There are various tools you can use for assessment, and some you may like to consider are:

- Giving yourself 'formal' tests (for example vocabulary tests).
- Getting someone else to 'test' your progress (for example, a fellow student, a native speaker of your chosen language, or a language teacher if you can find one). If you have a native speaker accessible, they will be able to assess your proficiency in speaking with a correct accent or tonality.
- Sitting down and thinking through what you have achieved - this is more subjective than objective assessment, but nevertheless useful.
- Looking back at your specific goals and seeing which ones you have achieved and to what standard (this can be ticking boxes or a fuller analysis of what you have done).

ACTIVITY
Create a learning Mind Map® for yourself

- Get some coloured pens - at least three colours.

- Also get a sheet of paper - preferably one that is larger than A4 - and turn it to 'landscape' (long side horizontal).

- Put in a central theme - 'What I have learned so far'. You are going to create a Mind Map®, using key words, that will remind you of the different things you have learned from this book so far.

- You may choose to have a key word for each section heading, or you may choose to have a key word for random things that come to mind.

- Having put in the initial key words, expand on the first concept by adding more detail - again in key words.

- Make it colourful - add pictures (they don't have to be works of art)!

Key learning point from step fifteen
- Assessment is a vital aid to ensuring that you are achieving your goals

Section Three
Communication techniques

Now you have had all the information on *how* to learn, we can come to some more specific guidance on *what* to learn. We are going to cover:

- Increasing your understanding of language types.
- Improving your specific spoken language skills.
- Improving your specific written language skills.
- Improving your non-verbal communications skills.

The purpose of this section is to give you some key skills that relate to language learning. Because there are so many languages, with so many differences, we aren't going to talk about any language in particular, but the guidance we will give you can be applied to whichever language you choose to learn. Let's take each of the areas in turn:

Step Sixteen
Increasing your understanding of language types

This section will cover:
- Language types.
- Language structures and grammar.
- Culture.

Language types

Languages differ in many ways and some of the key differences are as follows:

Spoken language

The sound of different languages varies tremendously. Some languages rely very much on differences in pitch, tonality or accentuation to express differences in meaning. In English, for example, you may say a sentence with your voice going up at the end, which denotes a question, or down at the end which denotes a statement, but this does not change the meaning of the words themselves. In other languages, however, the way you make sounds actually changes the meaning of the word - so correct pronunciation is much more important than in a language such as English.

You will also need to learn which words to stress in a sentence and also the rhythm to speak in.

EXAMPLE

People attending a Welsh language class fell into two main categories - those who had been brought up with no exposure to Welsh speaking, and those who had been brought up in a family and environment where Welsh was spoken, even though they, personally didn't speak it. The latter people sounded so much better when speaking Welsh sentences in the class as, although they were equally unfamiliar with the language as the other members of the class, they had absorbed the language rhythms and intonation from their family and therefore had the basic language sounds already - they only needed to apply them to the new words.

So, when you are learning, you need to pay attention to how you sound when you speak. This is particularly important if you are learning a language where correct tonality is vital and, in this case, we recommend you spend as much time as possible, early on, with native speakers of your chosen language and in listening to audio-programmes on that language, or in going to lessons with a professional teacher of that language.

EXERCISE

- Find a native speaker - preferably a child.

- Get the child to do what parents do with their babies. Engage the child in games which, co-incidentally, will benefit you too.

- Spend a number of sessions not talking at all.

- Simply get the child to touch his or her ear, saying what he or she is doing. As s/he does that, you do it too.

- Then get the child to touch his or her toes saying what s/he is doing. You do it too.

- Then get the child to touch objects, saying what s/he is doing. You do it too.

- Continue to play for as long as the child is willing (the younger the child, the shorter the concentration span so you may only get 10-minute sessions), and take up this game on a regular basis - ideally daily.
- Eventually - after about 15-20 hours of this, start repeating what is being said to go with the actions. So as the child says: "I am touching the plate" you repeat: "I am touching the plate" as you do it too.

CASE STUDY

Tony is a retired builder who left school at 15. His school life was plagued with ear and throat problems. He always thought that he couldn't learn a language - until he bought a holiday flat in Spain 25 years ago. Spending long holidays there, he was soon speaking fluently. He says that his best teachers were the children in the apartment block, who always patiently corrected him. Later, when he went to work in France for six months at a time, he used every opportunity to speak the language and picked up French even more quickly than Spanish.

Written language

Some languages have alphabets (or letters) while others have symbols. Because English is alphabetical, most learners who have English as their native language find alphabetical languages easier to learn to read than languages with symbols. There are also different alphabets - for example Greek and Russian. And languages with symbols also differ, so there are many variations. Chinese is an example of a language using symbols.

You will only need to learn written language if you wish to read or write, rather than just speak, the language, but if you do want to be able to read and write in your chosen language, the more that language differs from your own in its written form, the longer task you will have ahead of you.

Language structures and grammar

The ability to discern the structure of language seems to be 'hard-wired' into our brains (see exercise below). Although there are differences in structures of language, most people have an innate ability to make sense of the structure of their own language very early on.

Different languages, however, can have very different grammatical forms. For example, in English, verbs tend to come near the beginning of sentences, so that the sense of the sentence can be gained very quickly. In some other European languages, however, the verb only comes at the end of the sentence, so you need to hear the entire sentence before being able to make sense of what the person is saying.

Also, some people find it easiest to learn a language when they learn the grammar, while others prefer a conversational approach, where they learn by actually speaking and don't think about the structure of the language. When young children learn their native language, they do so conversationally, so this would seem the 'best' approach to a new language, however, as adult learners, our perception of the world has developed and we have developed our own specific learning styles (as you will have found out from Steps Four and Five) and so 'immersion' in a language, rather than formal grammatical instruction, does not work for everyone.

If you decide that understanding the grammar of your chosen language is important to you, you can acquire grammar books on the subject or find audio-programmes or classes that will cover this.

While you can generally make yourself understood in a language without having the grammar absolutely correct, if you want to communicate for business or other professional purposes, it will be more important to get the grammar right.

And you should remember that social etiquette/convention may mean that, even though you have learned 'correct' grammar, this may not be what is used for all conversations - you may also need to learn 'common' forms of speech for day-to-day speech.

EXERCISE

First of all, take a look at this sentence:

The lirte flids trimpd rutty in the dlp

Now answer these questions:

1 What kind of flids?

2 How did the flids trimp?

3 Where did the flids trimp?

So what is the theory behind this activity? Let's go back to the sentence:

The lirte flids trimpd rutty in the dlp

You will have answered some or all of the questions we asked you about this sentence. However, the sentence itself does not actually mean anything. But your mind has created some sort of order, logic or response in order to answer the questions. This is because your brain actually has a sense of the structure of language, even though you may not be aware of it.

Having discovered this, be aware that your mind will *automatically* create sense when you are in an environment where you do not understand the language and/or the culture. This means that your mind will do some of your language-learning for you at an unconscious level. So now do the following activity and let your unconscious mind do the work for you:

Assuming you have already gained a rudimentary knowledge of your chosen language, get a native speaker to ask you questions to which the answer will be 'Yes' or 'No'. Again, this could be done with a child, but equally well with an adult. The idea is to take in the meaning of the questions through watching the 'body language' (see Step Nineteen) of the speaker. At this stage you do not know what the person is asking you, but at an unconscious level you are taking in far more than the words.

Remember how much fun it will be to get things wrong.....your native speaker will laugh with you. Do not encourage the native speaker to 'translate' for you at this point for you can simply enjoy immersing yourself in the simple language.

Now look at this next sentence and take a guess at what it says:

Mi hia piipl a aks if mi an yu no wiari chat

Given that your mind will attempt to make sense of something that is not familiar, this is an example of where there is sufficient familiarity to be able to made a shrewd guess at what is being said.

It is actually Creole, based on English spoken in the Caribbean. Translated it says:

"I hear people asking if I and you aren't weary of talking".

TIP

Trust your mind to give you help when it is needed.

ACTIVITY
Recognising patterns in languages

The purpose of this activity is to get you thinking about the language you are learning.

Below are some extremes associated with languages (separated by a dotted line). Consider your chosen language and mark on the continuum where you consider that language is placed. If you don't know some of the things that follow, you can either ignore those particular ones, or you can choose to do some research into them, which will help your studying even more.

An example:

Pictures..Words

Where, on this continuum do you consider the Chinese language is placed? Well, because the Chinese language consists of a series of pictorial representations, it is likely that it is to the far left of this continuum.

Another example:

Closed gestures..*Open gestures*

Where, on this continuum do you consider the Arab languages are placed?

It is known that Arabs have 'open' gestures and may sometimes feel threatened by closed ones such as folded arms - so that language would be placed very close to 'open gestures' on this continuum.

A third example:

Similar to other.......................................*Nothing like other*
languages   *languages*

Where is Spanish on this continuum?

We know that people who learn Portuguese find Spanish easy - as do Italians - the languages are similar. So Spanish is nearer to the 'similar to other languages'. Or is it? It is not similar to Greek - or German - or Japanese. So choose carefully.

Here are some more for you to judge for yourself. The place on the continuum can be anywhere on the line.

Lots of gestures.......................................*Very few gestures*

Lots of touching.......................................*Very little touching*
when speaking   *when speaking*

Emphasis on tone......................................*Little or no emphasis*
                                                         on tone

Alphabet easy to......................................*Alphabet not easy to*
understand   *understand*

Musical sound to......................................*Harsh sound to*
language   *language*

Similar to your..*Very different from*
native language   *your native language*

Culture

Languages are embedded in their particular cultures, or ways of life. This may include, for example, their religions, politics, art, food and customs. This means that it is really useful to learn about the culture at the same time as learning how to speak the language.

To learn about culture, there are lots of things you can do, including:

- Visit the country where the language is spoken.
- Read about that culture - both present-day and historical.
- Join a club or association for people of that culture or those interested in it.
- Go to exhibitions or trade fairs relating to that country.
- Watch films made in that country.
- Visit web-sites that are relevant to your studies.
- Find pen-friends from that country who will correspond with you.

And, when learning a language, remember that certain cultural elements are likely to be demonstrated in the language itself - for example a different way of addressing people with whom you are very close and those with whom you have a more formal relationship.

Getting these elements right is important. (Also see the piece on 'Mirror Neurons' in Part Eighteen.)

Key learning points from step sixteen

- Many languages sound very different from each other
- It's vital to listen to the sound of a language
- Some people like to learn the structure of a language through its grammar while others learn better by just 'picking up' the language
- Our minds can make sense out of nonsense
- Languages are embedded in cultures

Step Seventeen
Improving your language skills
Spoken language

This step will cover:

- Listening.

- Speaking/using your voice effectively.

Listening and speaking are absolutely inter-related. Listening has two aspects:

a) Taking in the sounds so that you can make sense of them.

b) Showing the person you are communicating with that you are paying attention to them.

Speaking is the key aspect of learning a language, as this is the major method by which you communicate with other people. There are also two aspects to speaking:

a) The physical element - how you actually make sounds.

b) The way in which you combine those sounds to make understandable words and sentences.

At this stage, we would like to introduce you to the work of a French doctor, Dr Alfred A Tomatis, an ear, nose and throat specialist, whose research and teaching has some fascinating elements. His work explains a) why some people find language learning easier than others and b) why people from some countries find it especially difficult to communicate with people from some other specific ones.

Two of the key areas that Tomatis believed were essential in language learning are:

- Being able to *hear* the sounds (especially the tones) of the language you are learning.

- Being able to *pronounce* the sounds - within the right time-frame - of the language.

Dr Tomatis, who died in 2001, made it his life's work to explore hearing. He said that people can't reproduce sounds that they can't hear. He also suggested that language teaching is founded on an inaccurate assumption - that all people hear in the same way.

Tomatis discovered that people differ in their range of hearing according to the language(s) they learned in childhood (which is a good reason to ensure that children get to hear several foreign languages in their early schooling). This seems to depend on the frequencies that different people can 'tune in to'.

CASE STUDY

In 1976 the Tomatis method was tested in a school in Belgium. One group had Tomatis training, while the other was taught English as usual. The Tomatis group performed very much better than the other group.

All languages use the same 'base tones', which range from 125 to 250 Hz; however languages also have 'overtones', which differ from language to language. English for example, uses a lot of high-pitch sounds (2,000-12,000 Hz), while French rarely uses such sounds, but uses mainly 1,000 - 2,000Hz. The main instrument producing these differences is the tongue, which can be placed in different positions in the mouth.

Our ears are most attuned to the frequencies of our native language and we find it difficult to hear foreign tones and, therefore, to pronounce them correctly or memorise them easily. To give some examples of how this works in practice, French people (1,000 - 2000 Hz) have considerable difficulty learning English from the British (2,000 - 12,000 Hz) but not from North Americans (750 - 3000 Hz). (Could that be another reason, apart from spelling, that the British and Americans are described as two nations divided by the same language?) Slav languages have a range of 100 - 8,000 Hz and Slav people have a reputation for mastering a wide variety of different languages.

Tomatis also discovered that, in the same way that people have eye and foot dominance, everyone has an ear dominance and that affects their listening abilities. If you are 'right-eared' you can process sounds more quickly than 'left-eared' people, which can also make a difference to how easily you learn a language.

Another language characteristic that Tomatis worked on was the length of sounds. Languages differ in the length of their syllables. For example, the average American syllable takes 75 milliseconds to pronounce, compared with 50 milliseconds for a French syllable, so Tomatis said you have to train your ears to react more rapidly if you want to speak a language with shorter syllables.

And Professor Tomatis also developed a method to learn the structure of a language more easily. Babies in the womb hear sounds, but they are distorted because they have to travel through amniotic fluid. The structure of the native language seems to be absorbed in this way and, to re-create this for a foreign language, a system is used whereby that language is also filtered to produce the same kind of sound frequencies found in the womb and then, gradually, the sounds are changed so they better represent the sounds heard in 'normal' listening, ie through the air.

Being unable to reproduce the sounds required for a second language can quickly lead to a loss of motivation, so knowing about these hearing differences is important and, if you are interested, you can find out more as there are Tomatis Centres in many countries. What the centres do is 'train your ears' by identifying which frequencies you can or can't hear well and then 'exercising' your ears by getting you to use an 'electronic ear', which relays frequencies that you can't yet hear well.

The electronic ear can help overcome various difficulties in language learning, dyslexia and stuttering; it can also re-train you to become 'right-ear dominant' and, as mentioned above, to re-create sounds similar to those heard in the womb, in order to learn a language in a very 'natural' way.

So the Tomatis method is a fascinating approach to language learning and you can find out more about it on the following web-site: www.tomatis.com.

Now let's move on to some specific listening and speaking skills:

A Chinese pictogram for listening
[ear (biggest element), you, eyes, undivided attention, heart]

Listening Skills

Listening is vital in face-to-face and telephone communications with other people. When you listen effectively, you can take in what the other person is saying and, importantly, you can show that you are listening, so that the other person feels involved and valued. Listening is particularly important in language learning.

Key factors in listening are:

Looking at the other person

This shows you are paying attention and also enables you to watch their expression and 'body-language'. It is especially important to watch the person's mouth if you are trying to make sense of what they are saying and this is even more important if you are hard of hearing. When looking at someone, be careful, however, to take account of the amount of direct eye contact (looking at their eyes) that you have with them. This is for two reasons:

1) Because some people find direct eye contact intimidating or embarrassing.

2) Because in some cultures direct eye contact is not acceptable and may be seen as aggressive or intrusive. If either of these reasons applies to the person you are speaking with, then avoid direct eye contact and substitute looking at their mouth instead or, in rare cases, avoid looking at their face at all.

Giving non-verbal signals of attention

This means showing you are listening by nodding, smiling, leaning forward or any other way of acknowledging the other person, apart from speaking. This supports conversation and shows you are interested in what is being communicated.

Making 'listening sounds'

This helps to keep continuity in a conversation, shows you are listening and - if you don't have a good vocabulary in your chosen language - can also keep a conversation going without needing much speech. Listening sounds can be sounds such as: 'mmmm' or 'uh-huh'; they can also include very short words of acknowledgment such as 'yes' or 'I see' (in the chosen language, of course)!

Acknowledging what the person has said

This means showing that you have taken in and understood the words spoken. You can acknowledge by:

1) Repeating what the person has said ("So you went to the sea-side yesterday").

2) Summarising what the person has said ("So you went to the sea-side, swam in the sea, had a meal with your friends and then came back in the evening").

3) Paraphrasing what the person said - used your own words to say the same thing ("So you went to the coast and had a nice day with your friends").

Acknowledging what has been said, particularly if you are speaking in a new language, helps both you and the other person to make sure you have understood each other.

ACTIVITY

Speak to a native speaker on the telephone (or on Skype on your computer).

On the telephone you can't see the body language. Consequently it is good practice in listening and practising understanding; this can help you learn:

• When to speak.

• When not to speak.

• When to end a conversation.

Speaking and using your voice effectively

This is a really important skill in learning a new language, because:

- Languages vary in the ways in which words are spoken.
- If your voice is not clear, what you say, and the meaning of what you say, may be lost.

Some key points in speaking are:

- Breathe deeply enough to take in sufficient air to allow you to speak properly and then speak as you breathe out (if you don't think this is important, try speaking while breathing in)!
- Project your voice sufficiently to be heard.
- Make sure you fully articulate each word. This means making the beginning, middle and end of each word clear.
- Pause briefly between sentences so that it is clear that you have moved on to a new thought.
- Listen to how native speakers form their words and then try to use the same way of speaking; this means using the different parts of your voice structures in the same way as them. Voice structures include your tongue, teeth and larynx (voice box).

EXERCISE
Talk to yourself

Bob is a keen cyclist and chooses to go on long cycle rides whatever the weather. As he cycles along, he describes the scent and the environment to himself, out loud, in his chosen language. He says: "Don't be frightened of talking to yourself".

EXERCISE
Have fun

Get together with one or more people who are also learning your chosen language.

Have some fun! Get the other people to be deliberately obtuse. Imagine you are:

- Lost in a city and need to find your way back home.
- Have a bad tummy ache (or anything else that is not immediately visible) and need to get to a doctor.
- Need to buy something that is not on display.
- Are a vegetarian and need to explain what you can and what you cannot eat. Act out each scenario, practising words and body language.

ACTIVITY
Language learning techniques used by space programmes

Find a native speaker and use their own language to ask questions. Let them respond in English. Their English response will show you how much they have understood. Using this method, there is more clarity than there might otherwise be, and both parties understand at least some of what is going on.

As a real-life example of this, on the Apollo-Soyuz space missions, the American astronauts spoke Russian, despite their minimal command of the language, and the Russians (with comparable lack of skill) spoke only English. This was an excellent compromise that enabled them to communicate effectively.

This section has covered different ways of learning to speak a language. It's worth emphasising here that you *can* learn a language without ever visiting the places where it is spoken, but you may wish to make visits, either to supplement your learning or as your main learning process.

If you do want to make visits, you can go on holidays on your own or with friends, to visit family, friends, pen-pals or Internet friends. You can go on language courses run abroad, live with a family, arrange work experience overseas (maybe through your employing organisation if you have a job), undertake some voluntary service (if you are 18 years or older) or do a house swap (look on the Internet to find organisations that arrange this). Many of the case histories in this book show that people's skills and understanding increased by leaps and bounds with total immersion in the country of their choice.

If you prefer not to visit your chosen country, there are some computer software language courses (such as Rosetta Stone - see Resource List), which give the effect of immersion with interactive pictures, videos and native speakers, plus voice recognition for feedback. These have been widely used to excellent effect.

Key learning points from step seventeen
- Listening and speaking are inter-related
- People tune into different frequencies when they listen
- We have dominant ears
- Listening is particularly important when learning a language
- It's important to show that you are listening by making signals and sounds

Step Eighteen
Improving your language skills
Written language

You may wish to learn a new language purely for conversational purposes, or you may want to be able to read and write it too. Some useful tips on reading and writing are:

- If the language uses the same alphabet as your own native language, you will already have a head-start in writing.

- If the alphabet is different, or symbols are used instead of letters, you will first need to learn the new characters or 'pictures'. You can build this into your learning plan as one of your goals.

- You can practise your reading and writing in many ways and here are just a couple of examples you might like to consider:

Reading

- Reading a daily newspaper in your chosen language (you can get these sent to you from the publishers, or you may be able to borrow them if you have access to a local centre or have contacts with native speakers living in your own country).

- Getting people to send you emails in your chosen language.

- Saying the words you are reading to yourself as you read; you can do this 'in your head', but it's more useful to do it out loud so you can also check your pronunciation, which will help with your spoken language too.

- If possible, get a native speaker to listen to you reading aloud and give you feedback on how you are doing.

EXERCISE

Find topics to read about, or listen to, in your chosen language, that interest you. Then, each time you listen to a native speaker, watch a television programme, listen to a radio programme or read any magazines or books - see if you can identify the grammatical elements used, such as verbs, nouns, adjectives, etc. And compare the structures used in spoken language with the structures used in written language and notice the similarities and differences.

Writing

- Keeping a daily diary in your chosen language - not necessarily a learning diary, but a diary of your daily activities, thoughts and interests.
- Writing letters to pen-pals in your chosen language.
- Keeping a web-log (blog).

EXERCISE

If you have difficulty with spelling, this exercise can help you both spell and memorise new vocabulary.

Being able to visualise, or see in your 'mind's eye', is important for this method. So, before we start, picture a green apple. If you find it hard to visualise the apple, you will need more help, as the ability to visualise is one of the most useful tools for fast learners.

To visualise, you don't have to see things photographically clear or like a movie, just start with the feeling of the apple and notice if that leads you to another sense - maybe the smell or the sound of biting into the apple. It may help to have a piece of green paper or an actual apple in front of you to help you to remember.

The more you involve all of your senses the more it will help your learning and wake up the one(s) you are not using.

Once you can 'see' a green apple, you can move to the activity itself:

1) Take a piece of card or stiff paper. Write down the word that you want to learn to spell in your chosen language. This works for a range of scripts, such as Cyrillic, Chinese/Japanese and Arabic. Make sure that you have the correct spelling. Where appropriate, use lower-case characters as this makes the word more of an interesting shape.

2) Get into a comfortable position and think of something, someone or some place that makes you feel happy and at ease. Notice whereabouts in your body you feel that good feeling and then see whether you can make that feeling even stronger.

3) Switch off your internal dialogue (talking to yourself in your head). A good way to do this is to place the tip of your tongue on the roof of your mouth behind your front teeth.

4) Now look at the word that you know is spelt correctly; you might like to imagine you are taking a photograph of it. As you do this, you are making an association between feeling good and the correct spelling. Now imagine you are tracing around the outline of the word with your nose.

5) When you are ready, move the piece of paper from the table and hold it up and to your left. (Some people are more comfortable with the spelling up and to the right, so you can try each side in turn with this exercise and notice which works best for you.) Reinforce the good feeling as you see the target word there. When you are sure that you 'have it', move the paper away so that you are just visualising the word instead of reading it on the paper.

6) If, after you move it away, you 'lose' the spelling - just bring back the paper and have another look. If you have a long word and the middle looks a bit 'faded or wobbly' imagine that you have a control knob that can improve or strengthen the image.

7) Keep the good feeling as you visualise the word. Then simply copy the spelling from the visualisation on to a piece of paper on your desk or table.

8) Check back with the original spelling. Check each letter. If there is a single mistake, cross the whole thing out and go back to Step 1. You want to remember only the correct spelling.

9) One way to check that you are visualising is to write the word backwards as well as forwards.

If you have a list of spellings or vocabulary to learn, pin them high up and to the left on your wall or doorway - you can then just glance up and feel good as you look at them.

The strategies used by good spellers were discovered by NLP author and trainer Robert Dilts and further refined by Cricket Kemp of NLP NorthEast.

EXERCISE

Some things to learn

Here are a few specific things that will help you make progress quickly:

- Learn about 200 of the most frequently used nouns in your chosen language.
- Learn numbers up to 100.
- Learn the names of coins and paper currency.
- Learn a few common phrases. While you are still at the early stages of learning a new language and have been picking up a lot of information, it may also be useful to go to your phrase-book and learn some useful phrases and questions.

You will, for instance, go a long way by knowing how to be courteous, so learn:

- Hello.
- Goodbye.
- Thank you.
- Good morning/afternoon/evening.

And to help you

- I don't understand.
- Speak more slowly please.

Then there are the questions which, inevitably, will occur when you start engaging with native speakers:

- What is your name?
- How much is that?
- How do I get to….?
- What time will we meet?

And then there are the questions that will help you to pursue interests that you have. It is well worth spending some time considering what it is you really want to find out about, and jotting down some questions, and then looking up how you ask them in your chosen language. This activity will give a real boost to your ability to interact with native speakers.

Key learning points from step eighteen

- Reading anything in your chosen language will enhance your learning
- Writing a diary in your chosen language will also enhance your learning
- Anyone can learn to spell

Step Nineteen
Improving your non-verbal communication skills

Non-verbal communications are all the things you do with your body (your posture, your movement, your gestures and your facial expression). These give messages to people you are with and can either support or contradict your spoken messages. Sometimes non-verbal communications are called 'body language'.

Some specific non-verbal communications are:

- Smiling.
- Frowning.
- Nodding.
- Tapping your feet.
- Blinking.
- Shrugging your shoulders.
- Putting your head to one side.
- Leaning forward.
- Folding your arms.
- Making gestures with your hands.
- Turning your body to one side.

And there are lots more, including the differing use of 'personal space', whereby people in some cultures (including the UK), prefer to stand further from others in conversation, while in some other cultures people get much closer to each other when speaking.

When your body language supports your speech, you give a consistent message to people, but when it contradicts your speech (such as saying "I liked that place" while shaking your head), people get confusing messages.

Some body language tends to be common across most cultures, whereas some is very different. In some cultures, for example, shaking the head means 'no' but in others it means 'yes'. So when you are learning a language you do need to know how to support your spoken language with appropriate non-verbal body language, especially as non-verbal communications often carry more weight than spoken language.

CASE STUDY

The Independent newspaper reported that, in 1966, Virgin boss Richard Branson, in attempting a round-the-world hot-air-balloon flight, crash-landed in the Algerian desert in the middle of a civil war. He survived by making friends with a local warlord, who gave him food and drink as they chatted in pidgin French. Since they were speaking pidgin language, we have to assume that even more of the communication than normal was non-verbal. Branson has also made it known that he has dyxlexia, which can make learning foreign languages more difficult.

Some ways of building awareness of body language are by watching people, talking to native speakers, watching TV programmes, films and DVDs and visiting the country. When you are able to match these non-verbal communications, trust and rapport increase so that the exchange of messages becomes easier.

Try this experiment

Ask a group of friends: "What's that stuff that deaf people use?" while at the same time making movements in the air as if you are reading Braille with your fingers. If they answer: "Braille", you can point out that you mentioned people who were hard of hearing, not people who had difficulty seeing. Although you said one thing, your gestures (body language) were indicating another.

ACTIVITY

- When you watch a native speaker talking, either in live conversation or on a video or film, take particular notice of the actions that go with the words.
- Be aware of which actions almost always go with certain words or phrases.
- On your own, practise the words and phrases and be sure to make the gestures at the same time.

You are associating the gestures with the words in your brain and, by doing this, every time you use that word or phrase your procedural memory will lay down the path that will make the gestures quite automatic when you are using those words and phrases.

Mirror neurons

Exciting new research into how the brain works can help you be aware of non-verbal communications and learn a language.

Do you remember the last time you watched, and smiled, as you saw someone feeding ducks at the water's edge and that person was obviously getting great delight as they came to greet her? The researcher who found out about your ability to observe this - and to smile with recognition as you do, has called the neurons (brain cells) involved 'mirror neurons'.

When we recognise someone else's emotions, we are actually 'mirroring' the emotion of the other person. The purpose of the mirror neuron systems is to search out, watch, and interpret the actions of others, which allows us to build empathy or rapport. That interpretation includes understanding the actions, understanding the social meaning of the actions, and even developing a shrewd idea about the emotion that is being felt by the other person. However this interpretation is not cerebral - we are not reasoning when we interpret. We are 'feeling' what the other person is feeling.

This is particularly relevant to second language learning because, through these mirror neurons, we are able to 'feel' the cultural norms of people from other countries. We are not just learning words - we are learning about what makes the people 'tick'.

It has been further suggested that language is based on mirror neurons. The same neurological circuits that are used to move the tongue and the lips are used to make hand gestures, thus suggesting a connection between the two. So, when we speak, the likelihood is that our gestures are closely connected with our speech. This emphasises the importance of noticing, and copying the gestures, and lip movements, of native speakers when they are speaking. The new words you learn are not just new words - they are words combined with gestures - and feelings.

ACTIVITY

- Acquire a video, in your chosen language, that has a dramatic scene in it - a scene that evidently has emotions involved.
- Watch the actions, without the sound, and search out the feelings that are being portrayed.
- Turn up the sound and hear the sounds that go with the actions.
- Repeat the words, and include the gestures, as you watch.

This activity will help you both learn the language and learn the 'body language' that will help people understand you when you speak that language.

INTERESTING FACT

In February 2006 it was announced that the US military were funding the development of a language-learning game which concentrates on the development of appropriate body language. This is intended for use by troops trying to reduce the cultural divide between themselves and local people and in order to improve communication. Other games to be developed involve teaching the use of 'open' rather than 'closed' gestures, which can be perceived as aggressive. (Item reported on the BBC news website in February 2006).

Key learning points from step nineteen
- Your non-verbal communications give messages to others
- Our mirror neurons interpret the actions of others
- Undertake activities that motivate and interest you so you are encouraged to learn more

Step Twenty
Continuing to learn

In this book, we have given you ways of understanding how you learn, how to study and how to learn a language quickly and enjoyably. We hope you put this into practice and get the results you wish for.

We would also encourage you to continue finding out new ways to learn. Learning applies to every area of your life; it keeps your brain active and there is now evidence that continued learning and development can help create new brain cells and help avoid degenerative brain illnesses. So it's well worth continuing.

It's also important to continue learning because the world is constantly changing and, if we don't keep up with those changes, we may lag behind and fail to take advantage of new developments that present themselves.

And, you can also, of course, apply the techniques in this book to other areas of your life. If you want to develop any other new skill, then what you have learned here will help you - just adapt the activities to that skill and remember the key learning points that underpin them.

We wish you the very best for the future.

Appendix
Resource listing

We have mentioned various books, web-sites and other available resources in this book. In this Appendix you will find references to these, plus others that you should find useful.

Do take some time exploring the resources and also add others that you may come across yourself. All information can add to your learning and ability.

We have listed the resources in alphabetical order within each section.

Books

Anxiety Toolbox - Do You Put Your Life on Hold to Avoid the Situations That Scare You?
Thomas, Gloria (2004), published by Thorsons, UK.

Brain Gym for Business - Instant Brain Boosters for On-The-Job Success
Dennison, Gail, Dennison, Paul and Teplitz, Jerry (1994), published by Edu-Kinesthetics, USA.

Flow
Csikszentmihalyi, Mihaly (1992), published by Rider, UK.

Joyful Fluency - Brain-Compatible Second Language Acquisition
Freeman Dhority, Lynn with Jensen, Eric (1997), published by The Brain Store Inc. USA.

Lessons From the Art of Juggling - How to Achieve Your Full Potential in Business, Learning and Life
Gelb, Michael J and Buzan, Tony (1995), published by Aurum Press, UK.

Mind Your Language - A Practical Guide to Learning a Foreign Language
Nannetti, Remo L (2004), published by iUniverse, USA.

NLP Made Easy
Harris, Carol (2003), published by Thorsons, UK.

The Voice Book
McCallion, Michael (1988), published by Faber and Faber Limited.

ReDiscover Grammar
Crystal, David (9th impression 2003), published by Longman, UK.

Smart Moves - Why Learning is Not All in Your Head
Hannaford, Carla, published by Great Ocean Publishers, USA.

The Complete Guide to Learning a Language - How to Learn a Language With the Least Amount of Difficulty and the Most Amount of Fun
James, Gill (2003), published by howtobooks, UK.

The 20 Minute Break - Reduce Stress, Maximize Performance, Improve Health & Emotional Well-Being
Rossi, Ernest Lawrence PhD & Nimmons, David (1991), published by Jeremy P Tarcher Inc. USA.

The Test of Courage
Robbins, Christoper (2003) Biography of Michel Thomas (1914-2005), published by Hodder Arnold, UK.

Transforming Learning - Introducing Seal Approaches
Norman, Susan (Ed) (2003), published by SEAL (Society for Effective and Affective Learning), UK.

Use your Memory
Buzan, Tony (1995), published by BBC Books, UK.

Words That Change Minds - Mastering the Language of Influence
Charvet, Shelle Rose (2nd Edition 1999), published by Kendall Hunt Publishing, Canada.

Online Resources

The capability of the Internet is doubling every 18 months! There are numerous sites online that can help you with language learning. We have listed a few of these here. In addition, you can go to Google, or a similar search engine, and type in words such as 'Learn (insert your chosen language) free' and you will find much more. You can also try 'Non-verbal' (insert your chosen language) and you will find pictures of some of the important non-verbal gestures in that language.

Although the resources listed here were correct at the time of writing, it is possible that some may have changed in the intervening time.

www.acceleratedlearning.com/language/index.html
We recommend this type of course. They are only in French, German, Italian and Spanish however at the time of writing.

www.apple.com
Podcasts galore! Go to the Apple website and download 'itunes' software. Once you have the software on your computer look for 'podcasts'.

www.aussprachetraining.de/en/
This is to help pronunciation of German, but is relevant to all language learning.

www.bbcworldservice.com
A treasure-trove of information, with news and audio-clips in many languages (33 at the time of writing).

www.blogger.com/tour_start.g
A place to set up your own language learning web log or blog.

www.coe.int/portfolio
The purpose of the European Language Passport is to record and present language skills and cultural expertise crucial for learning and working in Europe. It was developed by the Council of Europe as part of the European Language Portfolio.

www.frenchpodclass.com/index.php?post_category=About
Unusual podcast for learning French.

www.michelthomas.com
French, German, Italian and Spanish courses.

www.nlpu.com
Encyclopaedia of NLP - Robert Dilts and Judith DeLozier - click onto 'encyclopaedia', explore language learning, NLP, non-verbal communication and more.

www.openuniversity.co.uk/power
The Open University offers courses in French, German and Spanish with books, audio visual and online aids, from beginner to degree level and with support from tutors throughout the courses.

www.rosettastone.com
If you want to supplement your learning with a course, this company offers 29 languages. They have voice-recognition built in so you can identify if you are pronouncing well. Languages offered are: Arabic, Chinese (Mandarin), Danish, Dutch, English (UK), English (US), Farsi (Persian), French, German, Greek, Hebrew, Hindi, Indonesian, Italian, Japanese, Korean, Latin, Pashto, Polish, Portugese, Russian (BR), Spanish (Latin American), Spanish (Spain), Swahili, Swedish, Tagalog, Thai, Turkish, Vietnamese, Welsh.

www.thesoundlearningcentre.co.uk
A centre offering auditory integration training for language learning and language difficulties.

www.soundlistening.com/tomatis.htm
Tomatis Centres worldwide providing information and assistance regarding Dr Tomatis and his work.

www.tomatis.com
A list of Tomatis Centres worldwide - available in several languages.

www.speechinaction.com
Speech in Action-online or CDROM-based training package, for learning English only.

www.wikipedia.com
A free online encyclopaedia and dictionary, available in more than 20 languages. Try reading entries first in your native language and then in the language you are learning.

www.word2word.com
An excellent web site with lots of free information on languages. It includes online dictionaries and translators, free online language courses, free online translation services and various forums for discussion. The site also includes hundreds of links to other free online language courses. At the time of writing, the site covered the following 118 languages:

Abenaki, Afrikaans, Ainu, Albanian, Arabic, Aramaic, Armenian, Asturian, Basque, Bengali, Bosnian, Breton, Bukharic, Bulgarian, Burmese, Catalan, Cebuano, Chamorro, Cherokee, Chichewa, Chinese, Chinook, Cornish, Cree, Creole, Croatian, Czech, Dakota, Danish, Dutch, English, Esperanto, Estonian, Finnish, French, Frisian, Friulian, Gaelic, Galician, German, Greek, Gujarati, Haida, Halkomelem, Hawaiian, Hebrew, Hiligaynon, Hindi, Hmong, Hungarian, Icelandic, Igbo, Indonesian, Italian, Ivatan, Japanese, Kannada, Kapampangam, Khmer, Kiribati, Konkani, Korean, Koyukon, Kurdish, Lao, Latin, Latvian, Lezgi, Lithuanian, Luganda, Malay, Malayalam, Maltese, Mandinka, Marathi, Michif, Mingo, Mon, Norwegian, Ojibwe, Pali, Papiamentu, Persian, Polish, Portugese, Punjabi, Quechua, Romanian, Rotuman, Russian, Samoan, Sanskrit, Sesotho, Serbian, Sicilian, Sinhala, Slovak, Slovenian, Somali, Spanish, Swahili, Swedish, Tagalog, Tahitian, Tamil, Telugu, Thai, Tibetan, Tigrigna, Turkish, Szotzil, Ukrainian, Urdu, Vietnamese, Waray-Waray, Welsh, Wollof, Xhosa.

If you go to these languages on the site, you will find a range of links to sites with general language information, lessons, grammar, history of language, tutorials, basic phrases, interactive activities, reading, pronunciation, language clubs and much more.

Also:

iTube!
The largest resource available for viewing Internet television, with over 1,000 channels of TV, live video channels and webcams, plus an Internet video search with over 2 million videos. Ideal for people learning languages. This needs to be purchased as inexpensive software, available from a number of different sources on the Internet.

Useful Organisations

Abebooks

www.abebooks.co.uk
A good Internet source of second-hand books on all kinds of subjects. If you need a specific book on a particular language you wish to learn, this could be a useful place to search for it.

Anglo-American Books

www.anglo-american.co.uk
A supplier of a wide range of books on learning and music to learn by.

Embassies

Contact embassies of the countries of the language you are studying to find out about conferences, films and cultural events in your area.

Instituto Cervantes

www.londres.cervantes.es; email:cenlon@cervantes.es; Tel: 020 7235 0353
Official Spanish Government Language Centre. Promotes Spanish language teaching and knowledge of the cultures of Spanish speaking countries throughout the world.

SCOLA

www.scola.org
A non-profit organisation that receives and re-transmits television programmes from around the world in native languages. It also provides other language-learning content via the website. SCOLA content is available via satellite, the Internet and cable providers.

SEAL

The Society For Effective and Affective Learning - www.seal.org.uk
email: seal@seal.org.uk
Holds biannual conference on learning - many members are language teachers.

The French Institute

Institute Francais - www.institut-francais.org.uk/elsewhere
email: info@ambafrance,org.uk; Tel: 020 7073 1350
Newsletter, multi-media library, French language courses, cinema; library.

The Goethe Institute

www.goethe.de/enindex.htm; Tel: 020 7596 4000
German language classes, library, films and cultural events.

The School of Oriental and African Studies (SOAS), London
www.soas.ac.uk
The only higher education institution in the UK specialising in the study of Asian and African languages. It also offers individual tuition and intensive courses during the University holidays.

Universities
Most universities around the world have a language learning departments with courses for adult learners Many are now offering websites and podcasts with a great deal of free information. Try typing the name of your nearest university into Google or another search engine.

Voice Care Network
www.voicecare.org.uk; email: info@voicecare.org.uk

Useful methods for helping with learning difficulties
Many people would learn languages more easily if they could overcome various learning issues they have. For example, some people have phobias about language learning, or have beliefs that they cannot learn, or have dyslexia, or find it hard to concentrate.

There are many ways of overcoming learning difficulties and we have given you many of them in this book. If, however, you need more, in-depth, help, we suggest you contact a professional practitioner who can assist you. There are many disciplines that are helpful in overcoming obstacles and we have listed some of these below. If you go an Internet search on these disciplines, you will find details of professional bodies and associations, details of individual practitioners and also further explanations of what each of the fields of study involve. Do make sure you check the skills and approach of whomever you consider working with - getting a list of accredited practitioners from the relevant professional body is a good start.

Brain Gym® (Educational Kinesiology)
A method of enhancing performance through specific body movements. For more information contact: www.braingym.org.

EFT (Emotional Freedom Technique)

A therapeutic tool for overcoming problems, involving light touch combined with eye movements to activate changes in brain response. You can find a free manual to teach yourself this tool at: www.eft.com. For more information contact one of the authors, Katrina Patterson via www.key2.demon.co.uk.

EMDR (Eye Movement Desensitisation Reprocessing)

Another therapeutic tool, using eye movements to make changes to brain reactions. For more information contact one of the authors of this book, Katrina Patterson, at: katrina@key2.demon.co.uk.

Hypnotherapy

A process that uses relaxation and suggestion to make changes to ingrained thoughts, feelings, beliefs and behaviours. For more information contact one of the authors of this book, Katrina Patterson, at: katrina@key2.demon.co.uk.

Life Coaching

Helping people sort out what they want in their lives and how to achieve the results they wish for. For more information contact one of the authors of this book, Penny Vingoe, via her web site: www.learntolearn.co.uk. She also offers coaching to adults, children and teachers who want to develop their learning ability.

NLP (Neuro-Linguistic Programming)

A kind of applied psychology that deals with the study of how people do things well. It helps people improve their performance by changing their behaviour, thoughts, feelings and beliefs. NLP has very rapid ways of overcoming phobias, but it's important to work through these with the help of a trained person. For more information contact one of the authors of this book via their web sites: Carol Harris: www.border.org.uk, Penny Vingoe: www.learntolearn.co.uk, Katrina Patterson: katrina@key2.demon.co.uk.

TFT (Thought Field Therapy)

A therapeutic tool for overcoming problems and changing states, involving light touch to activate changes in brain response. To find therapists around the world, go to: www.atft.org/web-locator.html or contact one of the authors of this book, Katrina Patterson, at: katrina@key2.demon.co.uk.

The following six pages contain some diagrams that summarise many of the key points from the book. You may find them useful and may also want to add to them other points that you have found of help.

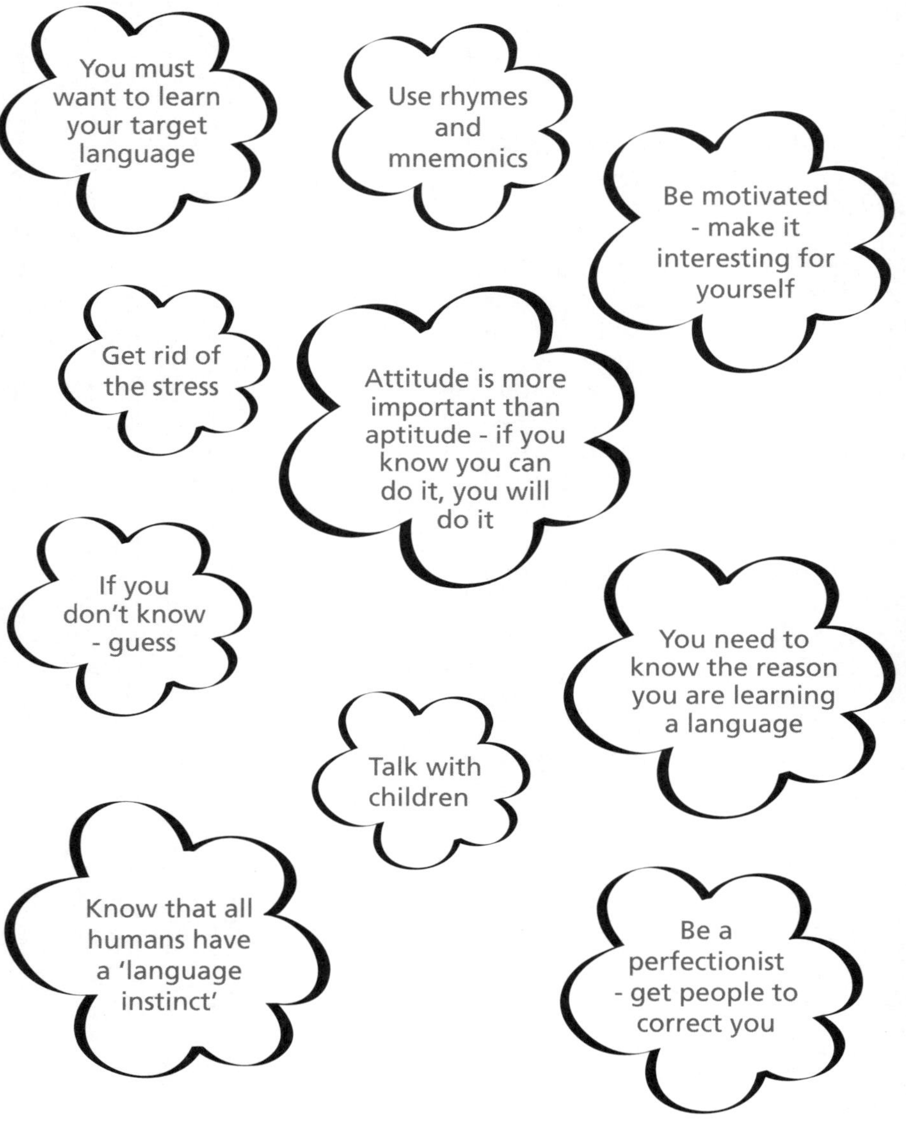

Act 'as if' you can speak the language
Have your own special learning space
Enjoy having fun and making a fool of yourself
If you plan you will focus - if you focus you are more likely to Learn
Make opportunities to enter into discussions
Your brain connects new ideas to those already in your head
Be so involved you haven't noticed the time passing
Use mind maps
Make understandable notes
Be consistent

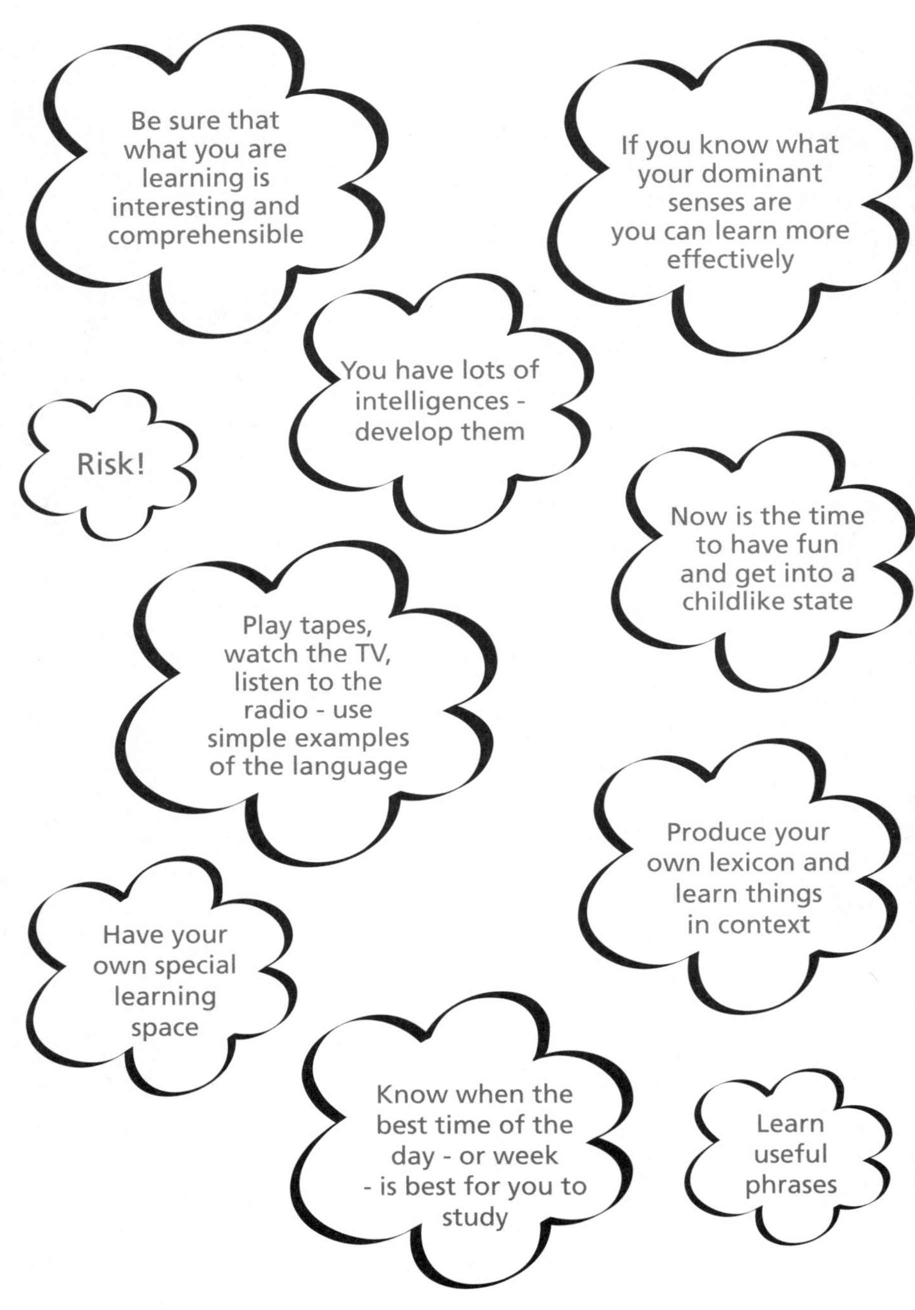

Be sure that what you are learning is interesting and comprehensible
If you know what your dominant senses are you can learn more effectively
You have lots of intelligences - develop them
Risk!
Now is the time to have fun and get into a childlike state
Play tapes, watch the TV, listen to the radio - use simple examples of the language
Produce your own lexicon and learn things in context
Have your own special learning space
Know when the best time of the day - or week - is best for you to study
Learn useful phrases

Read, read, and read some more - and read with a purpose
Listen to nursery rhymes
Be active - your learning is in your whole body
Practice makes perfect
Your mind and your body are connected
Make Puns
Use your computer
Put pictures - everywhere
Be aware of non verbal communication
Know that your unconscious mind is learning too
Your brain will look for meaning

Vocabulary is more important than accuracy
When learning grammar listen to examples until you know what you hear is right
Immerse yourself
If you can't make a mistake - you can't make anything
Leave each study session on a success
Picture new words
Once you have learned one second language, learning more will be even easier
Create structures for your memory
Love the culture the country of the target language
Be fascinated
Be purposeful

Carry your chosen language dictionary around with you
Create systems for your mind
Log your learning
Be healthy
Learning to spell correctly is easy
Repetition is the key to learning new words
Before you start to learn be in a positive state
The sooner you learn a little, the more motivated you are to carry on
Know what you want to achieve
Use voice recognition software

Authors' Biographies

Carol Harris has a degree in Sociology, is a Master Practitioner of NLP and was Chair of the Association for Neuro-Linguistic Programming. Her company, Management Magic, provides training, coaching, mentoring and facilitation to individuals and organisations. She is the author of a variety of books on topics including NLP, Management Consultancy, Networking, Magazine Production, Cookery, Weight Control and Pig Keeping! She has been involved as a Director of Studies with two UK schools for foreign students.

Katrina Patterson is a Certified Trainer of NLP, an executive coach and a therapist, using Ericksonian Hypnotherapy and energy therapies (EMDR, TFT and EFT). She also teaches Natural Vision Improvement and NLP to language teachers. She is a sessional lecturer in the Psychology Department of Birkbeck College FCE, London University and speaks regularly at conferences around the world. She was a researcher for Which? magazine for over 20 years, where she worked on many pan-European and inernational research projects.

Penny Vingoe (M.Ed.) is an NLP Master Practitioner and Trainer. She has an eclectic background, including wide experience of change work and training. Her company, Learn to Learn, established in 1989, was started as a result of her over-riding interest in learning (Accelerated Learning in particular) and in enabling others to blossom. Having done developmental coaching with both children and adults for almost 30 years, she is now a Life and Confidence Coach.